GOD'S LOVE

R. C. SPROUL

GOD'S LOVE

HOW THE INFINITE GOD
CARES FOR HIS CHILDREN

David C Cook®

transforming lives together

GOD'S LOVE
Published by David C Cook
4050 Lee Vance View
Colorado Springs, CO 80918 U.S.A.

David C Cook Distribution Canada
55 Woodslee Avenue, Paris, Ontario, Canada N3L 3E5

David C Cook U.K., Kingsway Communications
Eastbourne, East Sussex BN23 6NT, England

The graphic circle C logo is a registered trademark of David C Cook.

The website addresses recommended throughout this book are offered as a
resource to you. These websites are not intended in any way to be or imply an
endorsement on the part of David C Cook, nor do we vouch for their content.

Unless otherwise noted, all Scripture quotations are taken from the
New King James Version®. Copyright © 1982 by Thomas Nelson, Inc.
Used by permission. All rights reserved. Isaiah 45:7 quote is taken
from the King James Version of the Bible. (Public Domain.)
The author has added italics to Scripture quotations for emphasis.

LCCN 2012941798
ISBN 978-1-4347-0422-1
eISBN 978-0-7814-0852-3

© 2012 R. C. Sproul
Published in association with the literary agency of Wolgemuth & Associates, Inc.
First edition published as *Loved by God* by Word Publishing
in 2001 © R. C. Sproul, ISBN 978-0-8499-1648-9

The Team: Alex Field, Nick Lee, Renada Arens, Karen Athen
Cover Design: Amy Konyndyk

Printed in the United States of America
Second Edition 2012

1 2 3 4 5 6 7 8 9 10

062912

To Vesta

CONTENTS

PREFACE

I cannot imagine many tasks more daunting than attempting to set forth an exposition of the love of God. It is a matter so majestic, so transcendent, and so sweet in its implications that I lack the ability to do it justice. My passion for many years has been to focus attention on the character and nature of God, particularly of God the Father. I have endeavored to set forth something of His holiness, His sovereignty, His grace, and His justice. But these subjects, though weighty, are vastly less difficult than the love of God.

Rather than providing an exhaustive study of the love of God, I am restricting myself in this work to vignettes of that love. I will stress how God's love relates to His other attributes and how His inherent love serves as the standard by which human love is to operate. I also will look at some of the problematic questions that arise with respect to the love of God, such as how His love relates to divine "hate" and how His love relates to the doctrine of election.

I am indebted to the work of D. A. Carson on the love of God and also to that of the English Puritans. I am especially indebted to Jonathan Edwards for the insights into divine love that he set forth in his book *Charity and Its Fruits*.

I am grateful for the assistance of Kathy Miskelly and Maureen Buchman in the preparation of the manuscript. I also want to thank my wife, Vesta, for her loving criticisms of the manuscript. Special thanks are in order to my editors and publishers at David C Cook and to my agent, Robert Wolgemuth. I must also mention that this book was written during a period of grief over the loss of my close friend and comrade Dr. James Montgomery Boice. He had an uncanny grasp of the things of God, which appreciation has now been vastly increased since he has moved from the dark glass to the unveiled glory of God.

—*R. C. Sproul*
Orlando, Florida
Soli Deo gloria

CHAPTER 1

GOD IS LOVE

Love. This simple, four-letter word is magical. Its very utterance conjures up a host of images that are as diverse as the tiny colored pieces of glass that are configured into dazzling patterns by a kaleidoscope. By a mere turn of the tube, the glass pieces tumble into new arrangements. But magic depends on illusion for its potency; it has no real power. Likewise the empty word *love* can never evoke its reality. Indeed, the word staggers before its task of even describing the reality.

What is love? Is it the mystical essence exploited by the likes of Elmer Gantry, when he called it the inspiration of philosophers and the bright and morning star? Is it a warm feeling in the pit of the stomach associated with the sight of a cute puppy? Is it an attitude of acceptance that makes saying "I'm sorry" an unnecessary exercise? Is it a chemical response to the presence of an alluring member of the opposite sex?

If philosophers argue that the word *God* has suffered the death of a thousand qualifications, how much more must that be said of the word *love*? The elusive character of love has prompted far more than a thousand definitions. It has been used to describe so many things that its ability to describe a single thing has been sapped. A word that means everything obviously cannot mean anything. So, because the term *love* has been layered with so many diverse and sentimental associations, do we assume that it has lost all potency for communication and must be discarded to the scrap heap of useless vocabulary? By no means. The term is too rich and its usage so rooted in the history of human discourse that it would be catastrophic to abandon all hope of its reconstruction.

What is needed is the philosophy of the second glance, by which we look closely and carefully once again at what the word *love* signifies so we can separate the dross from the fine gold of its meaning. We need to distinguish between what *love* means and what it emphatically does not mean. This requires discerning the authentic from the counterfeit, the true from the false.

The problem we face is exacerbated when we realize that our interest is not limited to defining love in the abstract but defining it specifically as an attribute of God Himself. If we confess that love is an attribute of God, then our understanding of the nature of God is only as accurate as our understanding of the love we are attributing to Him. Neither may we retreat into a cavern of safety by declaring that although love is an attribute of God, it is not an important attribute, and therefore its distortion does no serious harm to our full understanding of God. Though it is a dangerous error to construct a hierarchy of attributes of God, the attribute of love is so important that if we do not get it right, we fail to have a sound understanding of God. Of course, that could also be said of the other attributes of God, such as His omniscience, immutability, infinity, and so on. In a word, all of the attributes of God are important. To say that His attribute of love is no more important than the others is not to say that it is less important or that it is unimportant. The Scriptures so clearly declare the importance of the love of God that to neglect it, negate it, or minimize it in any way would do violence to the sacred text.

To see how seriously the Bible takes the attribute of God's love, we need only to look at John's statement in his first epistle:

> Beloved, let us love one another, for love is of God; and everyone who loves is born of God and knows God. He who does not love does not know God, for God is love. In this the love of God was manifested toward us, that God has sent His only begotten Son into the world, that we might live through Him. In this is love, not that we loved God, but that He loved us and sent His Son to be the propitiation for our sins. Beloved, if God so loved us, we also ought to love one another. (4:7–11)

In this text, John made the remarkable assertion that "God is love." We notice immediately that he did not say simply that God is loving or that God loves. Rather, he said that God is love. What are we to make of this?

The word *is*, which is a form of the verb *to be*, sometimes forms a tautology. A tautology is the unnecessary repetition of an idea wherein there is nothing in the predicate that is not already present in the subject. For example, we could say, "A bachelor is an unmarried man." (This may also presuppose that the bachelor has never been married in order to distinguish him from a divorced man or from a widower.)

Was John stating the link between his subject, *God*, and his predicate, *love*, as an equation or an identification? I think not. If he had meant to declare an equation or identity, he would have said something like this: "God = love." Let us think for a moment about how an equal sign (=) functions in simple arithmetic. If we say that $4 + 3 = 7$, we see an equal identity on both sides of the equation. Nothing would be distorted if we reversed the order of the equation so that it read $7 = 4 + 3$. Essentially, there is no difference between 7 and $4 + 3$. They are identical in numerical value and content.

What would happen if we treated John's declaration in this manner? We could then reverse the subject and the predicate so that we could say either "God is love" or "Love is God." This is dangerous business indeed. If we can reverse the two sides of the equation, we can conclude that love is God. This could legitimize every conceivable heresy, including self-deification. If I have love, I must have God or actually be God. How easily we could move to exalting human eroticism to a divine plane, as indeed has happened with countless religions that have confused sexual pleasure with sacred devotion to God. The phenomenon of sacred prostitution flourished in ancient religions and is still practiced in modern cults. If one can do something in "love," it is blanketed with a divine sanction. It is clear that we do not want to infer from this text that any act of love is a divine act or that anything associated with our understanding of love must be of God.

At the same time, however, we do not want to dismiss lightly the dramatic statement John made in the text. He obviously had something important in mind when, under the inspiration of the Holy Spirit, he penned the words "God is love." At the very least, we conclude that what is being communicated here is that God, in His divine being and character, is so loving that we can say He *is* love. This would merely indicate emphasis, not necessarily identity.

We also could conclude that John was saying God is the fountain or source of all true love. This approach would be similar to how we would handle Jesus's statement that He is "the way, the truth, and the life" (John 14:6). Obviously, when Jesus spoke these words, He did not merely mean that He spoke the truth. Again, we face the question of equation or identity because of Jesus's juxtaposition of the verb *to be* with the predicate *truth*. If we reversed these, we would have to conclude that any truth is Jesus. This would mean the word *truth* means the same thing as the word *Jesus*. Rather than heading into such a linguistic morass, it is more appropriate to conclude that Jesus is the ultimate source, standard, or fountainhead of truth. This is how the Scriptures frequently speak of the relationship of God to things such as wisdom, beauty, knowledge, and goodness. God is not only wise; He is the ground of wisdom. He is not only beautiful; He is the source and standard of all beauty. He is not merely good; He is the norm of all goodness.

When we apply this manner of speaking to John's declaration that God is love, we see a literary device that points to God as the source, the ground, the norm, and fountainhead of all love. We recall that the biblical context in which John said "God is love" is an exhortation or commandment regarding how we are to behave toward one another. John wrote, "Beloved, let us love one another." This is the imperative before us. When John sought to provide a rationale for this commandment, he added, "For love is of God."

To say that love is *of* God means that love belongs to or is the possession of God. He possesses it as a property of His divine being, as an attribute. It also means that love is ultimately *from* God. Wherever love is manifested, it points back to its ground, its owner, and its source, God Himself. Again, this does not mean that all love is God, but it does mean that all genuine love proceeds from God and is rooted in Him.

The love John was describing obviously is not just a generic love. It is a particular kind of love. He spoke of it in restrictive terms. It is restricted to those who are born of God and who know God. He went on to say that the person who does not love in this restrictive sense does not know God and presumably is not born of God.

The restrictive type of love that characterizes God is awakened in those who have been born of God. It is a supernatural gift with a supernatural origin. It is found only in the regenerate, for all who exercise it and only those who exercise it are born of God.

DIVINE ATTRIBUTES

When we consider love as an attribute of God, we recognize that it is defined in relation to all the other attributes of God. This is true not only of love but also of every other attribute of God. It is important to remember that when we speak of the attributes of God, we are speaking of properties that cannot be bifurcated from one another.

One of the first affirmations we make about the nature of God is that He is not a *composite* being. Rather, we confess that God is a *simple* being. This does not mean that God is "easy" in the sense that a simple task is not a difficult task. Here, simplicity is not contrasted with difficulty but with composition. A being who is *composite* is made up of definite parts. As a human creature, I am composed of many parts, such as arms, legs, eyes, ears, lungs, etc. But God, as a simple being, is not made up of parts as we are.

This is crucial to any proper understanding of the nature of God. It means God is not partly immutable, partly omniscient, partly omnipotent, or partly infinite. He is not constructed of various segments of being that are assembled together to compose His whole being. It is not so much that God *has* attributes but that He *is* His attributes. In simple terms (as distinct from difficult terms), all of God's attributes help define all of His other attributes. For example, when we say God is immutable, we are also saying that His immutability is an eternal immutability, an omnipotent immutability, a holy immutability, a loving immutability, and so on. By the same token, His love is an immutable love, an eternal love, an omnipotent love, a holy love, and so forth.

By remembering that God is a simple being and that He is His attributes, we can resist the temptation of pitting one of God's attributes against another. God does not come to us like a chef who operates a smorgasbord restaurant. We cannot take our plates and help ourselves to only those attributes of God we find tasteful and pass by those attributes we find unpalatable. In practice, this is done every day. It is the basis of idolatry; we first deconstruct God by stripping Him of some of His attributes and then refashion Him into a different God more to our liking. An idol is a false god that serves as a substitute for the real God.

In antiquity and in contemporary primitive societies, we see idolatry practiced in crude forms. The idol maker who fashions a deity out of a block of stone or wood, then addresses it as if it is alive or has the power to do anything may seem somewhat foolish or stupid to us, for we live in more sophisticated times and are not quite as prone to worship the works of our hands in such a crass manner. But we have not yet escaped the propensity to worship idols created by our minds. We must guard against a facile dismissal of the threat of idolatry. We must remember that the proclivity for idolatry is one of the strongest inclinations of our fallen natures.

The Apostle Paul described the universal human need for salvation and spelled out the basis for the universality of human sin in his letter to the Romans:

> For the wrath of God is revealed from heaven against all ungodliness and unrighteousness of men, who suppress the truth in unrighteousness, because what may be known of God is manifest in them, for God has shown it to them. For since the creation of the world His invisible attributes are clearly seen, being understood by the things that are made, even His eternal power and Godhead, so that they are without excuse, because, although they knew God, they did not glorify Him as God, nor were thankful, but became futile in their thoughts, and their foolish hearts were darkened. Professing to be wise, they became fools, and changed

the glory of the incorruptible God into an image made like corruptible man—and birds and four-footed animals and creeping things.

Therefore God also gave them up to uncleanness, in the lusts of their hearts, to dishonor their bodies among themselves, who exchanged the truth of God for the lie, and worshiped and served the creature rather than the Creator, who is blessed forever. Amen. (1:18–25)

Here Paul spoke of the twin sins that are fundamental to fallen human nature: idolatry and ingratitude. By refusing to honor God as God, we substitute an idol for the true God. This is what is meant by exchanging the truth of God for a lie; such an exchange results in serving the creature rather than the Creator.

The need to be vigilant with respect to our natural instincts toward idolatry is especially acute when we are considering the love of God. I doubt there is another attribute of God more fraught with the peril of idolatry than this one. It is the attribute we most often select at our theological smorgasbord.

When I lecture on the holiness of God, the sovereignty of God, the justice of God, or the wrath of God, many times I am interrupted by someone who comments, "But my God is a God of love." I hasten to assure the person that I also believe in a God of love. But I often note in the protest a thinly veiled suggestion that the love of God is somehow incompatible with His holiness, sovereignty, justice, or wrath. These protesters isolate the attribute of love from God's other attributes so that it becomes the only attribute by which God is known. It subsumes or swallows up all of His other attributes.

This is precisely what happens when we conceive of God as a composite being rather than a simple one. We have a structure that allows us to pick and choose attributes, which gives us a license to construct a god who is an idol. If the Bible is our primary source for God's revelation of His nature and character, and it declares that God is holy, sovereign, just, and wrathful, as well as loving, we need to understand the love of God in such a way that it does not negate or swallow up these other attributes.

If we are to avoid a god who is an idol, it is imperative that we not only listen to what Scripture says about all of God's attributes, but also seek to understand each of those attributes in biblical terms. At this point, we encounter perhaps our greatest difficulty concerning the love of God. If we are to accurately understand God's love, then we must listen carefully to how God Himself defines love.

At the beginning of this chapter, I pointed out that our cultural definition of love is colored by a myriad of human feelings, passions, and concerns, which may have nothing to do with how the Bible describes love. Though the secular culture uses the word *love* just as the Bible does, this by no means indicates that the secular meaning of the term is identical to the biblical meaning. On the contrary, the two meanings are not only often different; they are often antithetical and incompatible.

Though the Bible uses the word *love* as a noun, it uses the word more often as a verb. That is, the Bible seems to be more concerned about what love does than what love is. In today's secular culture, the opposite is commonly the case. We tend to think of love more as a noun than as a verb. It is more often related to a feeling than an action. Of course, a feeling of affection is integral to the biblical concept of love, but that is not where the New Testament places the accent.

In secular usage, *love* is also more passive than active. Love is something that happens to us, something over which we have no control. We speak about "falling in love." We equate falling with an accidental action, not with a decision. We fall when we slip or are pushed or otherwise knocked over. The old ballad declared, "I didn't slip, I wasn't pushed, I *fell* ... in love." Another old standard celebrated the passive power of love with the words "Zing went the strings of my heart." Our heartstrings do not go "zing" because of a conscious decision of the mind to engage in a certain action. This view of love portrays it as a romantic episode that "comes over us" like influenza. It has a magical, romantic power that creates flutters in the heart, trembling in the knees, and flip-flops in the stomach.

On the other hand, the biblical view stresses the active side of love. For example, we are commanded to love not only our neighbor but even our enemy. How does one fall in love with an enemy? To love one's enemy presupposes that enmity is real. We really do have enemies, and we usually do not like them very much. But the command is not to *like* our enemies; it is to *love* them. But how can I love someone whom I do not like?

Sometimes lovers declare that they not only love each other but like each other as well. The cultural view of love suggests that it is possible to love without liking. That may be true if love is used as a synonym for a sexual or chemical attraction. But it makes no sense if love is defined in terms of personal affection. In that sense, love goes beyond and builds on liking.

To love our enemies means primarily that we behave in a loving way toward them. We treat them with the same kindness and integrity that we treat our friends. Herein is the active aspect of love. It is an *action* that is commanded by God, not a *feeling*.

Our actions reflect the kind of people we are. Activity flows out of being. What we are determines what we do. This is true not only for us but also for God. In theology, we distinguish between God's internal righteousness and His external righteousness. His internal righteousness is what He is in Himself. It is His being or nature. His external righteousness describes what God does. He always does what is right because, in one sense, that is all He is able to do. He can do only what is right because in His being He is altogether righteous. Because God is love, He is loving in His nature, and all of His actions reflect that love. As we will see later, there is a definite manner in which God is loving to His enemies even when they come under His judgment. When God commands us to love our enemies, He is not commanding us to do something that He refuses to do.

Just as God acts according to His nature, so do we. Indeed, that is our most critical problem. We are not sinners because we sin. Rather, we sin because we are sinners. In our fallen humanity, we are in such a state of corruption that to do what comes naturally is to sin. Jesus described this condition:

> Beware of false prophets, who come to you in sheep's clothing, but inwardly they are ravenous wolves. You will know them by their fruits. Do men gather grapes from thornbushes or figs from thistles? Even so, every good tree bears good fruit, but a bad tree bears bad

fruit. A good tree cannot bear bad fruit, nor can a bad tree bear good fruit. Every tree that does not bear good fruit is cut down and thrown into the fire. Therefore by their fruits you will know them. (Matt. 7:15–20)

Here Jesus declared that we cannot get good fruit from a bad tree or bad fruit from a good tree. The state of the fruit reveals the state of the tree. This connection is true in terms of the progress of our sanctification. When we are born from above and are indwelt by the Holy Spirit, we are at that moment conscripted by God for warfare. The instant we are reborn we are cast into a lifelong battle between the flesh and the spirit. Paul described that conflict:

I say then: Walk in the Spirit, and you shall not fulfill the lust of the flesh. For the flesh lusts against the Spirit, and the Spirit against the flesh; and these are contrary to one another, so that you do not do the things that you wish. But if you are led by the Spirit, you are not under the law.

Now the works of the flesh are evident, which are: adultery, fornication, uncleanness, lewdness, idolatry, sorcery, hatred, contentions, jealousies, outbursts of wrath, selfish ambitions, dissensions, heresies, envy, murders, drunkenness, revelries, and the like; of which I tell you beforehand, just as I also told you in time past, that those who practice such things will not inherit the kingdom of God.

But the fruit of the Spirit is love, joy, peace, long-suffering, kindness, goodness, faithfulness, gentleness, self-control. Against such there is no law. And those who are Christ's have crucified the flesh with its passions and desires. If we live in the Spirit, let us also walk in the Spirit. Let us not become conceited, provoking one another, envying one another. (Gal. 5:16–26)

In this passage Paul spoke of a contrast between the flesh and the spirit. The Greek word Paul used here for "flesh" may be used to distinguish the physical body from the soul, mind, or spirit of a person. However, especially when it is used in contrast with spirit, this word primarily refers not to our physical bodies but to our fallen, sinful natures. It is the word Jesus used when He told Nicodemus that it was necessary for a person to be born anew in order to see or to enter the kingdom of God (John 3:3, 5). He explained that in our first birth, our biological birth, we are born of and in the flesh. He said, "That which is born of the flesh is flesh." In contrast, the birth of the Spirit gives us a spiritual nature that we lacked before regeneration. Thus, Jesus also said, "That which is born of the Spirit is spirit" (John 3:6).

Only after we are born in the Spirit do we find ourselves locked in the struggle of which Paul wrote in Galatians. The combatants in this war are the flesh and the spirit. Again, this is not a battle between the body and the soul but between the old fallen nature of corruption and the new nature that has been wrought by the Holy Spirit's work of regeneration. Paul sometimes described this warfare as a battle between the "old man" and the "new man."

The Spirit's work of regeneration changes us radically. It liberates us from the bondage of sin. But regeneration does not instantly purify us. That occurs in our glorification, when our sanctification is completed. As Christians, we still sin. The old man is not annihilated at our rebirth. Our lifelong progress of sanctification involves putting to death the old man and nurturing and strengthening the new man.

Augustine used the comparison of a horse and its rider. He likened the unconverted person to a horse ridden by a single rider, the Devil. The converted person, however, is not ridden by a single rider. Rather, he is like a horse whose reins God and the Devil fight over.

This struggle between virtue and vice that is so common to us is utterly foreign to God. God is like a horse with only one rider. There is no conflict between flesh and spirit in Him. There is no gap between His internal righteousness and His external righteousness. The love by which He acts is altogether pure and untainted by any weakness, blemish, or hint of internal evil. If we learn nothing else about the love of God, it is imperative that we learn this. His love may be like our love in some respects, but in other respects it is unlike ours. Most significantly, our love is a marred love, a flawed and blemished love. Our love is always and everywhere tarnished by sin. That is why it is fatal to think of the love of God as a mere extension of human love.

We have seen that the attribute of love in God must be understood along with all of His other attributes. In this regard, we must stress that whatever else the love of God may be, first it is holy.

THE HOLY LOVE OF GOD

The word *holy* as it is used in Scripture has two chief meanings. The primary meaning refers to that which is transcendentally different from, or "other" than, creaturely things. That which is holy in this world has been set apart by or touched by the transcendentally holy. When God called to Moses from the burning bush in the wilderness, He commanded Moses to take off his shoes because he was standing on holy ground. What made the ground holy? It certainly was not the presence of Moses. What sanctified the ground was its intersection with the presence of God. The touch of God made it holy. The collision of the transcendent with the immanent, the sacred with the profane, transformed the ordinary into the extraordinary and the common into the uncommon. Palestine is called the Holy Land not because of the presence of the people of God, but because it was the arena of God's redemptive activity in history.

In this sense, the word *holy* refers to something that is "extra." It involves a certain plus that is added to the natural order. Holy space and holy time are so designated because something has been added to them. That which is added is the presence of God.

The second most frequent meaning of the word *holy* in the Bible is "purity." That which is holy has been cleansed from all impurity. This was expressed in the ritualistic cleansing rites of the Old Testament. For example, we see this established when God summoned Moses to Mount Sinai to receive the Law in Exodus 19:

> Then the LORD said to Moses, "Go to the people and consecrate them today and tomorrow, and let them wash their clothes. And let them be ready for the third day. For on the third day the LORD will come down upon Mount Sinai in the sight of all the people. You shall set bounds for the people all around, saying, 'Take

heed to yourselves that you do not go up to the mountain or touch its base. Whoever touches the mountain shall surely be put to death. Not a hand shall touch him, but he shall surely be stoned or shot with an arrow; whether man or beast, he shall not live.' When the trumpet sounds long, they shall come near the mountain." (vv. 10–13)

God's command that the people consecrate themselves by washing was based on the purpose He had expressed earlier when He told Moses that He had borne the children of Israel on eagles' wings and had brought them to Himself in the exodus. He said: "'Now therefore, if you will indeed obey My voice and keep My covenant, then you shall be a special treasure to Me above all people; for all the earth is Mine. And you shall be to Me a kingdom of priests and a holy nation.' These are the words which you shall speak to the children of Israel" (vv. 5–6).

The cleansing rite was commanded because God was calling Israel to be a holy nation. The status of holy nationhood was to be expressed by purity. When God calls His people to be holy because He is holy, they are to mirror His purity. We are not able to mirror His transcendence, but we are called to reflect His purity.

TRANSCENDENT LOVE

When we say that God's love is holy, we mean that it is both a transcendent love, an "other" kind of love, and a love that is absolutely pure. When we say God's love is holy in the transcendent sense, we mean that His love is different from ours. It has something extra, a "plus" that creaturely love lacks. This otherness is not total but is real and significant. The influence of Continental neoorthodox theology on the modern church has made it fashionable in some circles to speak of God as *wholly other*. This phrase was concocted to fight the influence of nineteenth-century liberal theology, which was moving toward pantheism to such a degree that the transcendence of God was being obscured and threatened. To overcome this threat and to reassert the importance of distinguishing God from the universe or from anything creaturely, the neoorthodox theologians insisted that God is not only "other" from the creation but that He is "wholly" other.

This effort to escape pantheism created a crisis in the language we use about God. One of the points that drove the "death of God" theology was the argument that human language is inadequate to speak meaningfully about God. Indeed, if God were absolutely different from us, utterly and completely "wholly other," human words could not express anything meaningful about Him. God could not reveal Himself to us, and we could spout only gibberish about Him. If two distinct beings have absolutely no point of commonality or similarity, they can have no meaningful communication. While we applaud the efforts of theologians to rescue the transcendence of God from the jaws of pantheism, we at the same time sound a sober warning against overreacting to the extent that we make it impossible to say anything meaningful about God, which would be the case if God were indeed wholly other. We must insist that God is *other* but not *wholly* other.

When we speak about God, we recognize that to a certain extent our speech is anthropomorphic and analogical. Anthropomorphic speech describes God in human forms. We see anthropomorphic language in the Bible when God is described as a sort of gigantic man or superman. He has a strong right arm (Ps. 89:13). He has eyes, ears, nostrils, and legs that use the earth as His footstool (Ps. 11:4; 2 Chron. 7:14; Ps. 18:9; Isa. 66:1). Yet as helpful as these images may be in revealing certain things about God, we are warned not to take them too far, as if they were univocal descriptions of Him. We are also told that He is not a man but a spirit who cannot be contained in time and space the way a physical being with real arms, legs, and eyes can be (2 Cor. 3:17).

When our language about God moves beyond graphic and concrete images (such as arms and legs) to more abstract language, we tend to think we have escaped the limits of anthropomorphic language. In fact, we never can. All of our language about God is always anthropomorphic because that is the only language at our disposal. It is the only language we have because we are *anthropoi*. God does not address us in His language. We could not understand it. Rather, He condescends to speak to us in our language. He reveals Himself to us in terms we can understand. As John Calvin once said, it is akin to the communication we use with infants. We coo and lisp to them in what we call baby talk.

I labor this point to make it clear that the only way we can speak of the love of God is anthropomorphically. However accurately we may speak about the love of God, our speech is limited by our human perspective. Whatever God's love is, it is not exhausted by our concept of it. It transcends our best efforts to describe it. It is higher than our loftiest notions of it.

When we say that our language about God is analogical, we mean that there is an analogy between who and what God is and who and what we are. Certainly there are important differences between the Creator and the creature. God is transcendent. He is other, but, again, not wholly other. A point of contact remains between God and man, a point of similarity between the Creator and the creature.

In classic theology, this point of similarity has been described as the *analogy of being* (*analogia entis*) between God and man. This analogy of being is rooted and grounded in creation itself. We see it in the creation narrative:

> Then God said, "Let Us make man in Our image, according to Our likeness; let them have dominion over the fish of the sea, over the birds of the air, and over the cattle, over all the earth and over every creeping thing that creeps on the earth." So God created man in His own image; in the image of God He created him; male and female He created them. Then God blessed them, and God said to them, "Be fruitful and multiply; fill the earth and subdue it; have dominion over the fish of the sea, over the birds of the air, and over every living thing that moves on the earth." (Gen. 1:26–28)

Genesis declares that we are created in the image and likeness of God. It is precisely because we are made in God's image that some point of similarity exists between us. It is this comparable image that makes meaningful communication between God and us possible.

Though God remains transcendent and our human language cannot exhaustively comprehend His love, nevertheless we can learn meaningful truth about His love from His revelation to us concerning it. That is what we will explore in the pages to come. We will approach the matter from two angles. On the one hand, we will look at what Scripture expressly says about the love of God. On the other hand, we will also look at what the Bible says about our human love, since in it we have an analogy of God's love.

CHAPTER 2
ETERNAL LOVE

Holy Scripture begins with five simple words, words that may be the most provocative and controversial words in the Bible: "In the beginning God created …" These words are controversial because they assert three crucial truths. They assert that there was a beginning to the universe, that there is a God, and that God is the Creator of the universe. These words stand in bold defiance to any theory of cosmology that teaches an eternal universe, a godless universe, or a self-created universe. Let us examine these three assertions more closely.

IN THE BEGINNING

When Genesis speaks of a beginning, it is referring to the advent of the universe in time and space. It is not positing a beginning to

God but a beginning to the creative work of God. One of the most enigmatic questions of philosophy and theology relates to the nature of time. Was the universe created *in* time, or was it created along *with* time? Did time exist before creation, or did it come into being with creation? Most classical theologians affirm that time correlates with creation. That is, before matter was created, time, at least as we know it, did not exist. How one approaches this question of the origin of time is usually bound up with how one understands the nature of time. Some see time not as an objective reality but merely as a category or construction of the mind.

However we conceive of time, we can agree that the ordinary manner by which we measure time requires a relationship between matter and motion. A simple clock uses hands that move around the face of a dial. We measure time by the motion of these hands. Or we may use an hourglass, which measures time by the passing of sand through a narrow aperture in the glass. The sundial measures time by the movement of a shadow. There are many devices to measure time, but in the final analysis they all rely on some sort of motion relative to some type of matter.

If there is no matter, we cannot measure motion. If we cannot measure motion, we cannot measure time. However, just because we cannot measure time without matter does not mean that without matter time does not exist. Genesis merely asserts that the universe had a beginning. It does not explicitly declare that time began with the universe. That concept is derived via speculative philosophy. The philosophical concerns are usually linked to our broader understanding of the nature of God. Especially when we declare with Scripture that God is eternal, the question of His relationship to time arises. Does His eternality mean that He is somehow outside of time, that He is timeless? Or does His eternality mean that He exists in an endless dimension of time?

However we answer this question, we conclude that God Himself never had a beginning. He exists infinitely with respect to space and eternally with respect to time. His existence has neither a starting point nor an ending point. The dimensions of His existence are from everlasting to everlasting. This means that He always has been and always will be.

IN THE BEGINNING *GOD*

Because God Himself had no beginning, He was already there in the beginning. He antedates the created order. When we affirm that God is eternal, we are also saying that He possesses the attribute of *aseity*, or self-existence. This means that God eternally has existed of Himself and in Himself. He is not a contingent being. He did not derive from some other source. He is not dependent on any power outside Himself in order to exist. He has no father or mother. He is not an effect of some antecedent cause. In a word, He is not a creature. No creature has the power of being in and of itself. All creatures are contingent, derived, and dependent. This is the essence of their creatureliness.

IN THE BEGINNING GOD *CREATED*

Thinkers hostile to theism have sought every means imaginable to provide a rational alternative to the notion of an eternal, self-existent deity. Some have argued for an eternal universe, though with great difficulty. Usually the temporal beginning of the universe is granted, but with a reluctance to assign its cause to an eternal, self-existent being. The usual alternative is some sort of self-creation, which, in whatever form it takes, falls into irrationality and absurdity. To assert the self-creation of anything is to leap into the abyss of the absurd because for something to create itself, it would have had to exist before it existed to do the job. It would have had to *be* and *not be* at the same time and in the same relationship. Some speak of self-creation in terms of spontaneous generation, which is just another name for self-creation. This would involve the logically impossible event of something coming from nothing. If there ever was a time when absolutely nothing existed, all there could possibly be now is nothing. Even that statement is problematic because there can never *be* nothing; if nothing ever *was*, then it would be something and not nothing.

Understanding the eternality of God is important because without some understanding of this attribute, our understanding of the love of God is impoverished. This is so because the love of God must be understood as an eternal love. Just as He is from everlasting to everlasting, so His love is from everlasting to everlasting. His is not a fickle love that waxes hot and cold over time. His love has a constancy about it that transcends all human forms of love. Just as human beings often fall in love, they also often fall out of love. This is not the case with God.

If God's love is eternal, we must ask whom or what did God love from all eternity? What was the *object* of that love? In the first instance, we see that God's eternal love had Himself as both the subject and the object of His love. As the subject, God did the loving. Yet at the same time, He was the object of His own love. Though this love was a kind of self-love, it was by no means a selfish love.

THE COVENANT OF REDEMPTION

Throughout the Scriptures, we encounter the making of covenants—agreements or contracts between people and also between God and people. We think immediately of the covenants God made with Abraham, with Moses, and with David. We think also of the new covenant that Jesus instituted in the upper room. All of these covenants, as well as others, have great importance in the outworking of God's plan of redemption.

The most important covenant, the one that precedes and forms the basis for all other covenants, is known in theology as the covenant of redemption. The covenant of redemption is rooted and grounded in eternity. It is a covenant within the Godhead, among all three persons of the Trinity.

The importance of the covenant of redemption is that it precludes any notion of the members of the Godhead ever working at cross-purposes. From all eternity, the Father, the Son, and the Holy Spirit agreed on the eternal plan of redemption. Before the world was created and before the human race fell, God knew that He would create and that there would be a fall. But God also knew that He would redeem His fallen creation and His fallen creatures. He knew from eternity that He would send His Son into the world to accomplish the task of redemption. He also knew that together with His

Son He would send the Holy Spirit into the world to apply the work of the Son to the elect.

. Sometimes the divine work of redemption is viewed as the resolution of a passionate struggle between the Father and the Son. The idea is that God the Father is a wrathful, vengeful God who has no interest in saving His creatures, only in condemning them. But God the Son, who is merciful and loving, persuades the Father to redeem His fallen children through the vicarious work of the Son. This notion has been prevalent throughout church history as people have tried to pit the Jesus of the New Testament against the Yahweh of the Old Testament.

This notion must be categorically rejected because it ignores the plain teaching of the New Testament, as well as that of the Old Testament. God the Father sends the Son into the world. This means that the incarnation, with its redemptive purpose, is certainly agreeable to the Father. Yet even though the Son is sent by the Father, the Son comes willingly. We see this in Paul's teaching in Philippians 2:

> Let this mind be in you which was also in Christ Jesus, who, being in the form of God, did not consider it robbery to be equal with God, but made Himself of no reputation, taking the form of a bondservant, and coming in the likeness of men. And being found in appearance as a man, He humbled Himself and became obedient to the point of death, even the death of the cross. Therefore God also has highly exalted Him and given Him the name which is above every name, that

at the name of Jesus every knee should bow, of those in heaven, and of those on earth, and of those under the earth, and that every tongue should confess that Jesus Christ is Lord, to the glory of God the Father. (vv. 5–11)

That Christ did not grasp or cling tenaciously to His prerogatives as God is seen by His willingness to lay aside His exalted status and embrace the humiliation inherent in incarnation. He willingly made Himself of no reputation in our behalf. Again, it was not as though the Father stripped His Son of His divine reputation against the Son's will. Not only was the Son consumed with zeal for His Father's house during His incarnation (John 2:17), but that consuming passion was His from all eternity (Ps. 69:9). Because of the Son's love for the Father, it has always been the Son's "meat and drink" to do the will of the Father. Likewise, when the Father set about to accomplish our redemption, He sent His Son whom He loved.

THE SON OF THE FATHER'S LOVE

It is generally understood that much of the history of Israel is recapitulated in the life and ministry of Christ. For instance, we see a striking parallel between the Old Testament episode of the sacrifice of Isaac on Mount Moriah and the sacrifice of Christ on Mount Calvary. We read in Genesis: "Now it came to pass after these things that God tested Abraham, and said to him, 'Abraham!' And he said, 'Here I am.' Then He said, 'Take now your son, your only son Isaac, whom you love, and go to the land of Moriah, and offer him there as a burnt offering on one of the mountains of which I shall tell you'" (22:1–2).

We notice that when God called Abraham, He instructed him to take his *son*, his *only* son, the one whom he *loved*, *Isaac*. God could not have been more specific. Had He spoken in general terms to Abraham and merely commanded him to sacrifice his son, it is virtually certain that Abraham would have searched out Ishmael and taken him to Mount Moriah. But God specified that the son he was to take was his only son, his only begotten from his wife, Sarah. It was further stipulated that the son to be sacrificed was the son Abraham loved. By this time, the addition of the specific name to the description was virtually superfluous. By now, Abraham clearly understood that God intended his son Isaac.

We see the parallel here with the Father's sending of His Son, Jesus, into the world. The Son whom the Father sent was His only begotten Son. It was the Son He loved, Jesus. Since Jesus was the Father's only begotten, there were no other sons from which to choose.

The main difference between the sacrifice of Isaac by Abraham and the sacrifice of Jesus by the Father was that at the last minute God gave Abraham a reprieve from his dreadful task and provided a lamb as a substitute for Isaac. The Father gave Himself no such last-minute reprieve. No substitute was provided for Jesus. He was the Lamb. He was the Substitute for whom there could be no other substitute. That Jesus was beloved of the Father is seen not only by the witness of the human authors of Scripture, who, under the inspiration of the Holy Spirit, gave us the written Word of God, but also in God's audible declaration from heaven. In Matthew's account of the baptism of Jesus we read:

> Then Jesus came from Galilee to John at the Jordan to be baptized by him. And John tried to prevent Him, saying, "I need to be baptized by You, and are You coming to me?" But Jesus answered and said to him, "Permit it to be so now, for thus it is fitting for us to fulfill all righteousness." Then he allowed Him. When He had been baptized, Jesus came up immediately from the water; and behold, the heavens were opened to Him, and He saw the Spirit of God descending like a dove and alighting upon Him. And suddenly a voice came from heaven, saying, "This is My beloved Son, in whom I am well pleased." (3:13–17)

It seems that even though God entrusted His Word to the inspired agents of revelation He chose and superintended to write the Bible, He reserved for Himself the right to make a public announcement from heaven, an *audible* announcement concerning the identity of Jesus. Jesus's baptism marked the beginning of His public ministry, the inauguration of His messianic vocation. At His baptism, He was anointed by the Holy Spirit for the task that was before Him. This moment marked the fulfillment of Isaiah's prophecy:

> The Spirit of the Lord GOD is upon Me,
> Because the LORD has anointed Me
> To preach good tidings to the poor;

He has sent Me to heal the brokenhearted,

To proclaim liberty to the captives,

And the opening of the prison to those who are bound;

To proclaim the acceptable year of the LORD,

And the day of vengeance of our God;

To comfort all who mourn,

To console those who mourn in Zion,

To give them beauty for ashes,

The oil of joy for mourning,

The garment of praise for the spirit of heaviness;

That they may be called trees of righteousness,

The planting of the LORD, that He may be glorified.

    (61:1–3)

From heaven, at this moment of the divine ordination of Jesus, the Father declared that Jesus was His Son. This relationship was challenged by the onslaught of Satan just a short time later in the Judean wilderness. At the heart of the satanic attack was the question of the authenticity of Jesus's sonship. Satan couched his seductive temptations within the framework of the question "*If* You are the Son of God …" The last words Jesus had heard before the Spirit drove Him into the wilderness to be tempted were the words from heaven declaring that He *was* the Son of God.

It is not enough for us to see that God declared Jesus to be His Son. He asserted two other things about Jesus at the same time. The first was that Jesus was His "beloved" Son. The second was that the Father was "well pleased" with His Son. The beloved Son of God was the object of the Father's affection. The Father Himself was pleased by His Son. There is no hint here of any tension between the disposition of the Father and that of the Son.

The Gospels record three occasions when God spoke audibly from heaven. In each of these episodes, God made a declaration concerning His Son. In two of them, He directly declared that Jesus is His beloved Son. The first occasion was at Jesus's baptism. The second was at His transfiguration shortly before the end of His public ministry:

> Now after six days Jesus took Peter, James, and John his brother, led them up on a high mountain by themselves; and He was transfigured before them. His face shone like the sun, and His clothes became as white as the light. And behold, Moses and Elijah appeared to them, talking with Him. Then Peter answered and said to Jesus, "Lord, it is good for us to be here; if You wish, let us make here three tabernacles: one for You, one for Moses, and one for Elijah."
>
> While he was still speaking, behold, a bright cloud overshadowed them; and suddenly a voice came out of the cloud, saying, "This is My beloved Son, in whom I am well pleased. Hear Him!" And when the disciples heard it, they fell on their faces and were greatly afraid. But Jesus came and touched them and said, "Arise, and do not be afraid." When they had lifted up their eyes, they saw no one but Jesus only.
>
> Now as they came down from the mountain, Jesus commanded them, saying, "Tell the vision to no one until the Son of Man is risen from the dead." (Matt. 17:1–9)

On this occasion, the announcement that was made at His baptism was repeated, with the addition of the admonition "Hear Him!" Peter spoke of this event in his second letter:

> For we did not follow cunningly devised fables when we made known to you the power and coming of our Lord Jesus Christ, but were eyewitnesses of His majesty. For He received from God the Father honor and glory when such a voice came to Him from the Excellent Glory: "This is My beloved Son, in whom I am well pleased." And we heard this voice which came from heaven when we were with Him on the holy mountain.
>
> And so we have the prophetic word confirmed, which you do well to heed as a light that shines in a dark place, until the day dawns and the morning star rises in your hearts; knowing this first, that no prophecy of Scripture is of any private interpretation, for prophecy never came by the will of man, but holy men of God spoke as they were moved by the Holy Spirit. (1:16–21)

THE ADOPTIONIST HERESY

One of the greatest threats to the Christian community in the early centuries was the adoptionist heresy. It reached its strongest point with the advocacy of Arius, who denied the deity of Christ and subsequently the doctrine of the Trinity. He held the position that Christ was not eternal but was the first and most exalted creature, and that He was adopted by the Father into sonship.

At the Council of Nicaea in 325, the adoptionist heresy of Arius was condemned, and the church embraced the full Trinitarian theology expressed in the Nicene Creed. The creed says of Christ that He was "begotten, not made." These words indicate that the council did not interpret the biblical language of begottenness to mean that the second person of the Trinity had a beginning in time. The word *begotten* refers not to origin but to the relationship that exists between the first person of the Trinity (the Father) and the second person of the Trinity (the Son).

The Council of Nicaea also declared that Christ is the eternal Son of God. That is, not only is the second person of the Trinity eternal; He is eternally the Son. We could add that He is eternally the *beloved* Son of God. The title *Son* was seen as describing not an office or task but His nature. The Son is divine by nature; He is not merely the Son in terms of His historical mission. As the second person of the Trinity, He is coeternal and consubstantial with the Father.

Though the church categorically rejected adoptionism and affirmed not only the deity of Christ but also His eternal sonship, it nevertheless maintained the biblical principle of our adoption. We are the children of God only by adoption. Our sonship does not confer deity on us. However, in our adoption we share in the eternal love of God. We experience the eternal love of God because we are adopted in Christ, the natural Son, and we are loved in Him as well.

The New Testament sees a close link between the love of God and our adoption into His family. John wrote:

> Behold what manner of love the Father has bestowed on us, that we should be called children of God! Therefore the world does not know us, because it did not know Him. Beloved, now we are children of God; and it has not yet been revealed what we shall be, but we know that when He is revealed, we shall be like Him, for we shall see Him as He is. And everyone who has this hope in Him purifies himself, just as He is pure. (1 John 3:1–3)

John began this statement with an expression of Apostolic astonishment. He indicated that the manner of love that God pours out on us in calling us His children is extraordinary. When he asked what *manner* of love it is, his question was rhetorical. He was obviously stunned by the transcendent character of such love that would include within its scope our participation in the family of God.

The Apostle Paul elaborated on this theme:

> Therefore, brethren, we are debtors—not to the flesh, to live according to the flesh. For if you live according to the flesh you will die; but if by the Spirit you put to death the deeds of the body, you will live. For as many as are led by the Spirit of God, these are sons of God. For you did not receive the spirit of bondage again to fear, but you received the Spirit of adoption by whom we cry out, "Abba, Father." The Spirit Himself bears witness with our spirit that we are children of God, and if children, then heirs—heirs of God and joint heirs

with Christ, if indeed we suffer with Him, that we may also be glorified together. (Rom. 8:12–17)

In applying the work of redemption accomplished by Christ in our behalf, the Holy Spirit gives to us the Spirit of adoption, by whom we can cry, "Abba." This privilege is often taken for granted in the Christian world, and its astonishing reality is misunderstood. Because of the frequent use of the Lord's Prayer in the life of the church, we have grown accustomed to addressing God as "Father." We miss the radical character of this privilege.

Critical scholars argue that Jesus's use of the term *Father* for God was a serious departure from Jewish tradition. Though pious Jews in antiquity at times referred to God as "the Father," it was virtually unheard of to address God directly as "Father." It is argued that the first reference in extant Jewish literature to God as Father as a form of immediate address was in the tenth century AD. The notable exception to this is in the New Testament. In every prayer of Jesus that is recorded, save one, Jesus addressed God directly as "Father." Indeed, this is one of the things that incited His enemies' hostility toward Him. They understood that by His use of the title He was claiming a unique relationship to God, one that even implied His equality with God.

When we see the radical character of Jesus's departure from tradition, we begin to understand the significance of His invitation to His disciples, and through them to us, to begin prayers by calling God "Father." The privilege that was Christ's alone for all eternity was passed on to His disciples. This is not because we are the natural children of God. Only Christ is the natural child of God. Rather, it is because we have been adopted into the family of God. As Paul declared, this adoption is given by the Holy Spirit, but it is an adoption that is in Christ and because of Christ.

Because of our adoption, Christ is now our elder brother and the firstborn of those who shall be raised from the dead (Col. 1:18). Because of our adoption, we receive a legacy to which we have no title by nature. We have become the heirs of God by virtue of being joint heirs with Christ. By nature, Christ is the sole heir of the Father. By adoption, the inheritance is extended to us.

Again, the radical character of this adoption and the marvel of the Father's love it reveals have been cheapened by the widely scattered teaching that all people are by nature the children of God. Nineteenth-century liberal theology was fond of reducing the essence of Christianity to two fundamental tenets: the universal fatherhood of God and the universal brotherhood of man. Neither of these so-called essentials of Christianity is biblical. The Bible does not teach the universal fatherhood of God. Indeed, we are called children of the Devil by nature (John 8:44; Eph. 2:1–3). On one occasion, Paul said that "we are also His offspring" (Acts 17:28). However, he was quoting a pagan poet and indicating that in one sense we are the offspring of God, namely, in the sense that we have all been created by Him. But the fatherhood of God is restricted in the Bible to believers who are in Christ and therefore adopted into the family of God.

Neither does the Bible teach the universal brotherhood of man. What the Bible teaches is the universal neighborhood of man. All people are my neighbors, but not all are my brothers. The brotherhood is a special group of people who are united with each other by virtue of their union with Christ. All who are united with Christ are therefore united with each other as brothers and sisters in Him.

When John exhibited astonishment at the kind of love that would allow us to be called the children of God (1 John 3:1), it was because he had difficulty explaining why God would love us to this extent. While we may assume that the reason God loves us in this manner is that we are so lovely, such an assumption is as arrogant as it is fallacious. God does not love us because we are lovely. He loves us because Christ is lovely. He loves us in Christ.

ADOPTING LOVE

To illustrate this kind of transferred love, we look to the narrative of Mephibosheth, the crippled son of Jonathan, in the book of 2 Samuel. Mephibosheth was injured when news came from Jezreel that Saul and Jonathan were dead. Mephibosheth's nurse picked him up and began to flee. In her haste, she stumbled and dropped the boy. As a result, he was left crippled. Later in 2 Samuel, we hear more of Mephibosheth:

> Now David said, "Is there still anyone who is left of the house of Saul, that I may show him kindness for Jonathan's sake?"
>
> And there was a servant of the house of Saul whose name was Ziba. So when they had called him to David, the king said to him, "Are you Ziba?"
>
> He said, "At your service!"

Then the king said, "Is there not still someone of the house of Saul, to whom I may show the kindness of God?"

And Ziba said to the king, "There is still a son of Jonathan who is lame in his feet."

So the king said to him, "Where is he?"

And Ziba said to the king, "Indeed he is in the house of Machir the son of Ammiel, in Lo Debar."

Then King David sent and brought him out of the house of Machir the son of Ammiel, from Lo Debar.

Now when Mephibosheth the son of Jonathan, the son of Saul, had come to David, he fell on his face and prostrated himself. Then David said, "Mephibosheth?"

And he answered, "Here is your servant!"

So David said to him, "Do not fear, for I will surely show you kindness for Jonathan your father's sake, and will restore to you all the land of Saul your grandfather; and you shall eat bread at my table continually."

Then he bowed himself, and said, "What is your servant, that you should look upon such a dead dog as I?"

And the king called to Ziba, Saul's servant, and said to him, "I have given to your master's son all that belonged to Saul and to all his house. You therefore, and your sons and your servants, shall work the land for him, and you shall bring in the harvest, that your master's son may have food to eat. But Mephibosheth your master's son shall eat bread at my table always." (9:1–10)

The flight of Mephibosheth's nurse was clearly motivated by fear of David and his men. To secure the throne for David, his men had to make sure no heirs of Saul were left who might dispute David's kingship by claiming dynastic rights for themselves. David's view, on the other hand, was radically different. He was searching for heirs of Saul, not to slay them but to honor them. He was motivated to honor any surviving descendants of Saul not by his affection for Saul but by his love for Jonathan.

The relationship between David and Jonathan was based on an extraordinary love. Some cite this relationship as a biblical paradigm that legitimizes male homosexual love. However, nothing in the text suggests that the love between David and Jonathan was sexual in the slightest degree. It is possible for men to share a bond of brotherhood that never becomes sexual. There was a deep sense of loyalty between David and Jonathan.

The text of 1 Samuel says that Jonathan loved David as "he loved his own soul" (20:17). Later, David sought survivors from the house of Saul to show them kindness for Jonathan's sake. This kindness David described as the "kindness of God." It was a divine kindness that David wanted to show, a desire that was not rooted in any love David had for Mephibosheth but in David's love for Jonathan. Apparently David had not even met Mephibosheth before this moment.

Mephibosheth was obviously fearful on being brought into the presence of David. When he was brought before the king, he fell on his face and prostrated himself. This act was not a mere sign of obeisance before royalty; it was a sign of personal terror. David called on Mephibosheth to relax, saying, "Do not fear, for I will surely show you kindness for Jonathan your father's sake, and will restore to you all the land of Saul your grandfather; and you shall eat bread at my table continually."

Overwhelmed by this announcement, Mephibosheth cried out, "What is your servant, that you should look upon such a dead dog as I?" It is important to note here that the dog was not a favorite household pet among ancient Israelites, but was seen as a filthy scavenger with few redeeming qualities. Not only did Mephibosheth refer to himself as a dog, but he called himself a dead dog. This brings to mind the exchange between Jesus and the Syro-Phoenician woman in the New Testament, when Jesus said, "Let the children be filled first, for it is not good to take the children's bread and throw it to the little dogs." The woman replied, "Yes, Lord, yet even the little dogs under the table eat from the children's crumbs" (Mark 7:27–28).

In both of these narratives people describe themselves in self-abasing terms, willing to see themselves as dogs. They express an acute consciousness of not being worthy of the treatment they are receiving. For Mephibosheth, it included the privilege of being invited to eat regularly at the king's table. David declared, "He shall eat at my table like one of the king's sons" (2 Sam. 9:11). For all practical purposes, David adopted Mephibosheth. He gave him the same privileges and status accorded David's sons. Again, David's action was not motivated by pity for someone who was crippled. Neither was it motivated by anything inherently lovely about Mephibosheth. The whole motivation was rooted in David's profound love for Jonathan.

This narrative is a microcosm of redemption. All humankind has fallen. In a sense, we were injured when our nurses dropped us in a fall. The fall left us spiritually crippled, unable to walk the path of righteousness on our own. Yet we have been invited to come into the King's family as His adopted children and to eat at His table. Our adoption and privileged status in the King's house are rooted in the eternal love of the Father for His Son. We receive the benefits due the heir of the Father. Because of the Father's love for Christ, we are welcomed into His family. This point should register in our minds every time we participate in the Lord's Supper and come to the King's Communion table.

My father was known to be a generous man. He was quick to help people in need and those who had experienced serious reversals in their financial affairs. After his death, I was startled to receive unrequested and unexpected benefits from several of them. When I was in seminary, my wife and I were poor. Many weeks we subsisted on peanut-butter sandwiches. One afternoon I went to the mailbox, where I found an envelope with no canceled stamp on it. Inside the envelope was one hundred dollars in cash from a man I had not seen in more than ten years, but who had been helped by my father. That hundred dollars was the most needed windfall we have ever received. We received it for nothing we had done. We received it simply because I was my father's son and someone wanted to express his appreciation for my father.

The Old Testament prophet Jeremiah wept over the coming judgment of God. But in the midst of those times of trouble, God used Jeremiah to promise the coming of a new covenant and the redemption of a remnant from Israel:

> "At the same time," says the LORD, "I will be the God of
> all the families of Israel, and they shall be My people."

Thus says the LORD:

> "The people who survived the sword
> Found grace in the wilderness—
> Israel, when I went to give him rest."

> The LORD has appeared of old to me, saying:
> "Yes, I have loved you with an everlasting love;
> Therefore with lovingkindness I have drawn you.
> Again I will build you, and you shall be rebuilt,
> O virgin of Israel!
> You shall again be adorned with your tambourines,
> And shall go forth in the dances of those who rejoice.
> You shall yet plant vines on the mountains of Samaria;
> The planters shall plant and eat them as ordinary food.
> For there shall be a day
> When the watchmen will cry on Mount Ephraim,
> 'Arise, and let us go up to Zion.'" (Jer. 31:1–6)

God promises the restoration of His people based on a love that He describes as *everlasting*. The love of God for His redeemed is not only *from* everlasting; it is also *to* everlasting. It is a love without end, a love that never ceases. In this regard, the love that the Father has for His Son will be poured out on us forever. The preservation of a remnant gives rise to a new covenant:

> Behold, the days are coming, says the LORD, when
> I will make a new covenant with the house of Israel

and with the house of Judah—not according to the covenant that I made with their fathers in the day that I took them by the hand to lead them out of the land of Egypt, My covenant which they broke, though I was a husband to them, says the LORD. But this is the covenant that I will make with the house of Israel after those days, says the LORD: I will put My law in their minds, and write it on their hearts; and I will be their God, and they shall be My people. No more shall every man teach his neighbor, and every man his brother, saying, "Know the LORD," for they all shall know Me, from the least of them to the greatest of them, says the LORD. For I will forgive their iniquity, and their sin I will remember no more. (Jer. 31:31–34)

This new covenant promised here was to be new to the people but not to God. It was the historical expression that was made in eternity past among the members of the Godhead that would, in due course, manifest the eternal love of God.

CHAPTER 3

THE LOYAL LOVE
OF GOD

I once was seated on an airplane next to a famous businessman who owned several nationally known enterprises. During our conversation, I asked him what he regarded as the most important quality in a member of his management team. Without hesitation, he answered, "Loyalty."

I was surprised by this man's response. I thought he would put competence, creativity, or some other virtue ahead of loyalty. His answer smacked of a man who was looking for managers who would function simply as yes-men, sycophants who would never challenge his thinking.

As I explored the man's answer more deeply, it became clear that he was not looking for yes-men. He explained that he wanted competent people in his organization. But, he explained, though competency was at times difficult to find, it was not as rare as authentic loyalty. A loyal subordinate is not a yes-man, because to say yes when you think no is itself an act of disloyalty.

Every person who has experienced personal relationships of any significance has had some taste of disloyalty. To be mistreated by an enemy is to be expected. To be attacked by a friend is devastating. To experience betrayal at the hands of a close friend or a loved one is to suffer one of the most painful wounds in human relationships.

PAUL'S LOYALTY TO CHRIST

As the Apostle Paul neared the end of his life, he wrote what is thought to have been his final epistle, his second letter to his beloved disciple Timothy. Paul knew that he was about to be executed, we presume by the emperor Nero. Toward the end of this final letter, he penned these inspiring words: "For I am already being poured out as a drink offering, and the time of my departure is at hand. I have fought the good fight, I have finished the race, I have kept the faith. Finally, there is laid up for me the crown of righteousness, which the Lord, the righteous Judge, will give to me on that Day, and not to me only but also to all who have loved His appearing" (4:6–8).

With these words, Paul expressed his loyalty to Christ. He saw his death as just one more sacrifice of praise offered to his Lord. His death would be like an oblation, a liquid offering presented in worship and devotion. He recapped his life and ministry in terms of an ongoing battle, but the fight was not conducted with bitterness or aggression. His fight was a *good* fight, a righteous battle.

His next metaphor was borrowed from the world of sports. Like a marathon runner who is tempted to abandon the race when he is winded and his breath comes in tortuous gasps but who presses on, Paul finished the race Christ had set before him. Finally, he mentioned that in all these things he had kept the faith. By keeping *the* faith, Paul remained loyal to the teachings of Christ and to Christ Himself. It is significant that Paul said more than that he had kept faith. He had kept *the* faith.

The consequence of Paul's loyalty to Christ and the faith was that he was looking ahead to receiving a crown of righteousness that was in storage, waiting for the day when Jesus would present it to him.

This passage is inspiring because it exudes a sense of victory and hope that extends beyond the Apostle to every follower of Christ who is loyal to Him by fighting the good fight, finishing the race, and keeping the faith.

PAUL EXPERIENCED BETRAYAL

What is shocking about this passage is that in the next verses Paul revealed that he had been deeply hurt by several of his earthly comrades:

> Be diligent to come to me quickly; for Demas has forsaken me, having loved this present world, and has departed for Thessalonica—Crescens for Galatia, Titus

for Dalmatia. Only Luke is with me. Get Mark and bring him with you, for he is useful to me for ministry. And Tychicus I have sent to Ephesus. Bring the cloak that I left with Carpus at Troas when you come—and the books, especially the parchments.

Alexander the coppersmith did me much harm. May the Lord repay him according to his works. You also must beware of him, for he has greatly resisted our words.

At my first defense no one stood with me, but all forsook me. (vv. 9–16)

Paul mentioned that Demas had forsaken him. This Demas was certainly not a casual acquaintance of Paul. We meet him in Colossians 4:14 and in verse 24 of Philemon. Demas was identified as a colaborer with Paul and one who was present with him during his first Roman imprisonment. It is clear that Demas shared some trials with Paul and had been part of his inner circle of friends. Then, at the crisis moment in Paul's life, his friend Demas deserted him. He left Paul for love, but it was not for the love of Paul or the love of Christ. It was the love of this present world. By deserting Paul, Demas at the same time deserted Christ for the things of this world. Whether he ever repented and returned to Christ is left untold in the biblical record. But Demas was not the only one to betray Paul. He mentioned that at his first defense no one stood with him; all forsook him. Imagine the visceral feeling of a man who had endured the hardships Paul had endured, who had poured out his life as a sacrifice, only to be abandoned in his darkest hour by his comrades.

The tragedy is that this experience is not all that unusual. Augustine suffered a similar fate near the end of his life, and countless others in ministry have endured the same experience.

However painful it was for Paul to experience the disloyalty of his friends, it did not leave him in despair, because the "all" who forsook him did not quite include all. He wrote: "But the Lord stood with me and strengthened me, so that the message might be preached fully through me, and that all the Gentiles might hear. And I was delivered out of the mouth of the lion. And the Lord will deliver me from every evil work and preserve me for His heavenly kingdom. To Him be glory forever and ever. Amen!" (2 Tim. 4:17–18).

At the very moment Paul was experiencing the betrayal of his friends, he was also experiencing the presence of Christ. He said that the Lord stood with him and strengthened him.

Psalm 23 may be the best known of all the psalms. It says, in part, "Yea, though I walk through the valley of the shadow of death, I will fear no evil; for You are with me" (v. 4a). The psalmist did not say that God would keep him from having to walk through the valley of the shadow of death. Rather, the promise was that God would be present with him while he walked through that shadowy place. For Paul, the presence of Christ, as He stood with him, more than compensated for the desertion of his friends.

JESUS EXPERIENCED BETRAYAL

Neither was Jesus Himself a stranger to the desertion and betrayal of His friends. His betrayal at the hands of Judas and His denial by

Peter are well known. Yet when we examine the record closely, we see that Jesus was forsaken by more than Judas and Peter.

When Jesus entered into His passion, He experienced unspeakable torment in His soul. The narrative of His agony in the garden of Gethsemane bears graphic testimony to this. On the one hand, He wrestled in prayer with the Father, asking for the bitter cup that had been placed before Him to be removed. While He endured this trial of the soul, He made a simple request of His disciples: to stay with Him and watch. Yet, when He came to His disciples, He found them sleeping: "Then He came and found them sleeping, and said to Peter, 'Simon, are you sleeping? Could you not watch one hour? Watch and pray, lest you enter into temptation. The spirit indeed is willing, but the flesh is weak'" (Mark 14:37–38).

Jesus rebuked Peter for not being able to stay awake with Him for one hour. Peter could not remain loyal for sixty minutes. We note that this occurred before any soldiers had yet arrived in the garden. There was no immediate danger to Peter, no pressing emergency that called his attention elsewhere. Jesus did not ask Peter to drink His cup for Him or to bear the burden the Father had placed on Him. All He asked was for Peter to watch for Him while He withdrew to pray. Peter was to stand guard for Jesus in His darkest hour to that point.

One would think that after the embarrassment of being found asleep on his watch by his Lord and then being exhorted to watch and pray lest he enter into temptation, Peter would have been exceptionally vigilant and alert. Not so:

> Again He went away and prayed, and spoke the
> same words. And when He returned, He found them

asleep again, for their eyes were heavy; and they did not know what to answer Him. Then He came the third time and said to them, "Are you still sleeping and resting? It is enough! The hour has come; behold, the Son of Man is being betrayed into the hands of sinners. Rise, let us be going. See, My betrayer is at hand." (vv. 39–42)

Jesus returned to His personal agony, leaving Peter to watch again. When He returned, He found Peter and the other disciples asleep again. A third time the result was the same, and Jesus said, "It is enough!" Three times He was left to wrestle with God alone while His trusted friends took a nap.

There is irony in this text. It focuses on Jesus's use of the word *hour*. He declared that the hour had come. On several occasions during His ministry, Jesus had spoken of His hour. For instance, at the wedding feast of Cana, Jesus rebuked His mother for pushing Him to address the host's predicament of running out of wine. He said to her, "Woman, what does your concern have to do with Me? My hour has not yet come" (John 2:4).

Usually when Jesus referred to His hour, He was speaking of His hour of suffering and death. On other occasions, He referred to His future hour of exaltation. In the passion narrative, however, His hour clearly referred to His hour of suffering. This was the hour that had cast a dark shadow over His entire life. It was the hour for which He was preparing Himself not only in Gethsemane but also during His entire public ministry. This hour was not a period of a mere sixty minutes. It was to continue until His death.

It is against the backdrop of this hour of supreme agony that the simple "hour" of Simon's watch is contrasted. His hour of betrayal, his sixty-minute disloyalty, intersected with the paranormal hour of the passion of Christ.

During the night, the betrayal of Jesus at the hands of men was exacerbated. First Judas appeared with the soldiers sent to arrest Jesus. He betrayed Jesus with his infamous kiss, the original kiss of death. The record of the arrest in the garden is punctuated by a terse conclusion: "Then they all forsook Him and fled" (Mark 14:50). The disciples awoke from their naps in time to gird themselves for their flight from Jesus.

While Jesus was taken for His trial, Peter was busy fulfilling Jesus's prediction of denial:

> Now as Peter was below in the courtyard, one of the servant girls of the high priest came. And when she saw Peter warming himself, she looked at him and said, "You also were with Jesus of Nazareth."
>
> But he denied it, saying, "I neither know nor understand what you are saying." And he went out on the porch, and a rooster crowed.
>
> And the servant girl saw him again, and began to say to those who stood by, "This is one of them." But he denied it again.
>
> And a little later those who stood by said to Peter again, "Surely you are one of them; for you are a Galilean, and your speech shows it."
>
> Then he began to curse and swear, "I do not know this Man of whom you speak!"

A second time the rooster crowed. Then Peter called to mind the word that Jesus had said to him, "Before the rooster crows twice, you will deny Me three times." And when he thought about it, he wept. (Mark 14:66–72)

As shameful as Peter's denial was, it was not the only act of forsakenness that Jesus was to endure. He was betrayed by Pontius Pilate. During his interrogation by Pilate, Jesus was judged to be innocent of the charges brought against Him. Pilate publicly declared that he had found no fault in Jesus. Yet despite this belief, he surrendered to the bloodlust of the crowd that was screaming for Jesus's crucifixion. By pandering to the crowd, Pilate violated Roman law, his own office, and the prisoner who stood before him.

JESUS WAS CURSED BY GOD

It would seem that if a man is betrayed by His closest friends, by the legal authorities, and by the public, there would hardly be anyone left to forsake Him. But the nadir of Jesus's forsakenness was still to come. It was to come at the hands of God Himself.

One of the most poignant moments in all of biblical history came while Jesus was hanging on the cross. Darkness covered the earth, and Jesus screamed in agony:

Now when the sixth hour had come, there was darkness over the whole land until the ninth hour. And at the ninth hour Jesus cried out with a loud voice, saying, "Eloi, Eloi, lama sabachthani?" which is translated, "My God, My God, why have You forsaken Me?"

Some of those who stood by, when they heard that, said, "Look, He is calling for Elijah!" Then someone ran and filled a sponge full of sour wine, put it on a reed, and offered it to Him to drink, saying, "Let Him alone; let us see if Elijah will come to take Him down."

And Jesus cried out with a loud voice, and breathed His last.

Then the veil of the temple was torn in two from top to bottom. (Mark 15:33–38)

Jesus's screamed words are taken directly from Psalm 22: "My God, My God, why have You forsaken Me? Why are You so far from helping Me, and from the words of My groaning?" (v. 1).

The urgent question is, "Why did Jesus call out these words?" Was it merely to recite Hebrew poetry or to call the attention of the witnesses of His execution to the incredible literal fulfillment of the messianic psalm of David? Was it, as critics have argued, a cry of sudden panic that God might not vindicate Him in His messianic vocation? Did He merely *feel* forsaken while in reality He was not forsaken?

If we are to take the words of Jesus on the cross seriously and link them to the Apostolic understanding of His death, we must grant that Jesus not only felt forsaken but actually was forsaken. This forsakenness casts a shadow over the concept we are currently exploring, the loyal love of God. If God's love is the ultimate paradigm of loyal love, how can we explain the Father's dreadful breech of loyalty to His only begotten Son?

To understand this departure from loyalty, we must turn to the Apostolic explanation of what was going on during the crucifixion of Christ. Perhaps the clearest treatment of this is found in Paul's epistle to the Galatians:

> For as many as are of the works of the law are under the curse; for it is written, "Cursed is everyone who does not continue in all things which are written in the book of the law, to do them." But that no one is justified by the law in the sight of God is evident, for "the just shall live by faith." Yet the law is not of faith, but "the man who does them shall live by them."
>
> Christ has redeemed us from the curse of the law, having become a curse for us (for it is written, "Cursed is everyone who hangs on a tree"), that the blessing of Abraham might come upon the Gentiles in Christ Jesus, that we might receive the promise of the Spirit through faith. (3:10–14)

For Jesus to fulfill His mission of redemption, the mission that was conceived in eternity, He had to serve as a substitute for His people. His suffering was vicarious. His role as Messiah was to be the Suffering Servant of Israel, the Sin Bearer of His people. To complete that mission, He had to take on Himself the punishment that was due those whom He was representing. In terms of the old covenant, the sanctions were dual. There were the promise of blessing for obedience to the law and the promise of cursing for disobedience. Paul cited Deuteronomy to explain this. The larger text of Deuteronomy spelled it out as follows:

> But it shall come to pass, if you do not obey the voice of the LORD your God, to observe carefully all His commandments and His statutes which I command you today, that all these curses will come upon you and overtake you:
>
> Cursed shall you be in the city, and cursed shall you be in the country.
>
> Cursed shall be your basket and your kneading bowl.
>
> Cursed shall be the fruit of your body and the produce of your land, the increase of your cattle and the offspring of your flocks.
>
> Cursed shall you be when you come in, and cursed shall you be when you go out. (28:15–19)

The litany of curses cited here indicates that the penalty for disobeying God is to be under His curse in all things, in all ways, and in all places. The specific references to the curses here are not exhaustive, but illustrative. Deuteronomy gets more specific in the next section:

> The LORD will send on you cursing, confusion, and rebuke in all that you set your hand to do, until you are destroyed and until you perish quickly, because of the

wickedness of your doings in which you have forsaken Me. The LORD will make the plague cling to you until He has consumed you from the land which you are going to possess. The LORD will strike you with consumption, with fever, with inflammation, with severe burning fever, with the sword, with scorching, and with mildew; they shall pursue you until you perish. And your heavens which are over your head shall be bronze, and the earth which is under you shall be iron. The LORD will change the rain of your land to powder and dust; from the heaven it shall come down on you until you are destroyed.

The LORD will cause you to be defeated before your enemies; you shall go out one way against them and flee seven ways before them; and you shall become troublesome to all the kingdoms of the earth. Your carcasses shall be food for all the birds of the air and the beasts of the earth, and no one shall frighten them away. The LORD will strike you with the boils of Egypt, with tumors, with the scab, and with the itch, from which you cannot be healed. The LORD will strike you with madness and blindness and confusion of heart. And you shall grope at noonday, as a blind man gropes in darkness; you shall not prosper in your ways; you shall be only oppressed and plundered continually, and no one shall save you.

You shall betroth a wife, but another man shall lie with her. (vv. 20–30)

This grim description of the extent of the curse is also partial. The text continues with gruesome details of the full measure of the curse.

THE BIBLICAL CONCEPT OF THE CURSE

The whole idea of a curse is lightly regarded in our culture. We tend to associate it with superstitious practices of primitive religions, such as the use of pins in voodoo dolls. But we cannot begin to grasp the significance of the cross or the full measure of the love of God without first having some idea of the biblical concept of the curse.

In biblical terms, the curse stands in direct contrast to the concept of blessing. In Old Testament literature, an important literary device is the oracle. The oracle was a way in which a prophet pronounced a divine revelation. Oracles were pronouncements of good news or bad news. The announcement of good news was an oracle of weal. An announcement of God's judgment was an oracle of woe. The oracle of weal was prefaced by the word *blessed*, as is seen in Jesus's oracles of weal called the Beatitudes. Conversely, the oracle of judgment was prefaced by the word *woe*, as Jesus used in His pronouncements against the scribes and Pharisees: "Woe to you, scribes and Pharisees, hypocrites ..." (Matt. 23:13).

Since the curse stands in direct antithesis to the blessing, we can better understand the significance of the curse by understanding first the concept of blessing. In the famous Hebrew benediction, we read: "And the LORD spoke to Moses, saying: 'Speak to Aaron and his sons, saying, "This is the way you shall bless the children of Israel.

Say to them: 'The LORD bless you and keep you; the LORD make His face shine upon you, and be gracious to you; the LORD lift up His countenance upon you, and give you peace'"'" (Num. 6:22–26).

The structure of this benediction is in the Hebrew poetic form of parallelism. There are three stanzas, each containing two points.

bless	keep
make face shine	be gracious
lift up His countenance	give peace

We see here an identity or synonymous parallelism on both sides. For example, the concept of blessedness is identified concretely with God's making His face to shine on a person and/or lifting up the light of His countenance on him. For the Jew, the highest possible state of blessedness was to experience the beatific vision, the direct sight of the face of God. Of course, in Old Testament terms, the direct vision of God was forbidden to fallen humans and was reserved for the saints in glory. But the closer one was to that ultimate condition, the greater the measure of blessedness. In other words, blessedness was measured in terms of the nearness of God to the individual and was accented by the notion of basking in the refulgent glory that shines out of His presence, the kind of glory evident in the *shekinah* that shone round about on the plains of Bethlehem the night Christ was born.

By contrast, the curse was related to the absence of God. To be cursed was to have God turn His back on you, to be removed from the blessedness of His presence, to enjoy not the light of His countenance but to be sent into outer darkness. The curse was measured in terms of the distance God was from you.

The curse of God was acted out in dramatic fashion on the Old Testament Day of Atonement:

> And when he has made an end of atoning for the Holy Place, the tabernacle of meeting, and the altar, he shall bring the live goat. Aaron shall lay both his hands on the head of the live goat, confess over it all the iniquities of the children of Israel, and all their transgressions, concerning all their sins, putting them on the head of the goat, and shall send it away into the wilderness by the hand of a suitable man. The goat shall bear on itself all their iniquities to an uninhabited land; and he shall release the goat in the wilderness. (Lev. 16:20–22)

After the blood of the sacrifice had been sprinkled on the mercy seat, attention was turned to the scapegoat. By laying his hands on the head of the goat, Aaron symbolically transferred or imputed the sins of the people to the goat. This goat was not slaughtered in the camp, where God had promised to be present and to meet with His people. Rather, the goat was driven into the wilderness, the place of outer darkness, which symbolized the place of cursing.

In His work of atonement, Christ fulfilled the role of the sacrificial lamb whose blood was poured out as an offering for sin. This was the work of propitiation by which Christ satisfied the demands of God's justice in our behalf. But Christ also fulfilled the role of the scapegoat, carrying our sins into the wilderness. This act was the work of expiation, by which our sins were removed or carried away from us by Christ. In this sense, Christ became a curse for us.

JESUS FULFILLED THE CURSE MOTIF

The drama of the New Testament fulfillment of the Old Testament Day of Atonement worked itself out in amazing detail. It was significant that Jesus was not killed by the Jewish authorities but by the Romans. For the curse to be fulfilled, the Messiah had to be delivered into the hands of the Gentiles, who were strangers to the covenant and were "outside the camp." This was the first step of the curse. The next step was that Jesus was taken outside the walls of Jerusalem to be executed. Here he was taken physically outside the "camp."

It is noteworthy that Christ's execution was not by the Jewish method of stoning but by the Roman manner of crucifixion. Paul alluded to this in Galatians when he referred to Christ's being hung on a tree, fulfilling the Old Testament curse for anyone who is hung on a tree (Gal. 3:13).

The curse motif is further evidenced by the astronomical phenomenon of God's plunging the world into darkness in the middle of the day.

But the fullest manifestation of the curse is found in Jesus's cry from the cross about being forsaken. To be cursed of God is to be forsaken by God. Jesus's cry was not merely an expression of disillusionment or an imagined sense of forsakenness. For Him to complete His work of redemption, He actually had to be forsaken. He had to receive the curse of the Father in His own person. The Father had to turn His back on His only begotten Son. The Father had to cover His face and not let Jesus see the light of His countenance.

The Apostles' Creed gives a brief summary of the life of Christ, which includes these words: "suffered under Pontius Pilate, was crucified, dead, and buried. He descended into hell." This reference to the descent into hell has been the subject of much debate. Some churches delete it from their recitation of the creed. Others place an asterisk by it and change the words to "he descended into death" or some other alternative. The earliest record of the phrase dates to the middle of the third century, which has led some scholars to conclude it was not in the original creed.

In dealing with this phrase, John Calvin argued that Jesus's real descent into hell did not occur after Jesus died but while He hung on the cross. Hell is the ultimate expression of the curse of God. For Jesus to be a curse for us, He had to endure the full measure of that curse, including the punishment of hell. Jesus experienced the fullness of hell while He was on the cross. His agony there had little to do with the physical pain of nails or thorns; it was the agony of bearing the wrath of God in its fullest sense that provoked the cries of the Redeemer.

Again we are faced with the question, how can we speak of the loyal love of God if He was willing to forsake His own Son? Any attempt to answer this question must begin where we began, back in eternity with the covenant of redemption. The Father's willingness to subject His beloved Son to forsakenness was matched by the Son's willingness to be forsaken in behalf of His people in order to secure their salvation. It is ironic indeed for parties to a covenant to agree on forsakenness, but that is the basis of our salvation.

The mode of redemption through suffering was forecast in the Suffering Servant passages written by the prophet Isaiah. In Isaiah 53, we read the following:

> Surely He has borne our griefs
> And carried our sorrows;
> Yet we esteemed Him stricken,
> Smitten by God, and afflicted.
> But He was wounded for our transgressions,
> He was bruised for our iniquities;
> The chastisement for our peace was upon Him,
> And by His stripes we are healed.
> All we like sheep have gone astray;
> We have turned, every one, to his own way;
> And the LORD has laid on Him the iniquity of us all.
>   (vv. 4–6)

The vicarious nature of the Servant's suffering is spelled out here. He bore our griefs, carried our sorrows, was wounded for our transgressions, was bruised for our iniquities, was chastised for our peace, and was lashed by the whip for our healing. The critical point to see here is that the One who smote and afflicted Him is God. It is God Himself who laid on the Servant, or imputed to Him, our iniquity.

At this point, the Father was not being disloyal in His love. On the contrary, He was maintaining His steadfast love, which He declared from the beginning.

Perhaps the most difficult sentiment to understand in this drama is found later in Isaiah 53:

> Yet it pleased the LORD to bruise Him;
>
> He has put Him to grief.
>
> When You make His soul an offering for sin,
>
> He shall see His seed, He shall prolong His days,
>
> And the pleasure of the LORD shall prosper in His hand.
>
> He shall see the labor of His soul, and be satisfied.
>
> By His knowledge My righteous Servant shall justify many,
>
> For He shall bear their iniquities. (vv. 10–11)

In what sense does Scripture speak of the pleasure of God when it says that "it *pleased* the LORD to bruise Him"? This does not mean that God took sadistic delight or diabolical pleasure in tormenting His beloved Son. The reference to pleasure indicates that the Father was pleased by the redemption that was accomplished in this manner. It pleased the Father that His Son was willing to give His life as a ransom for many. It pleased the Father that the Son was willing to make Himself of no reputation so we could be redeemed. It pleased the Father that the Son did not depart from the plan that had been conceived in eternity. The pleasure was in the redemption, not in the pain endured by the Son.

That the disposition of the Father was in favor of the Son and not against Him is shown by several factors. The first is Jesus's own statement. Despite His full exposure to the forsakenness of the Father, in Jesus's last breath of life, after declaring that the atoning work was finished, He committed His spirit into the Father's hands: "Now it was about the sixth hour, and there was darkness over all the earth until the ninth hour. Then the sun was darkened, and the veil of the temple was torn in two. And when Jesus had cried out with a loud voice, He said, 'Father, "into Your hands I commit My spirit."' Having said this, He breathed His last" (Luke 23:44–46).

If the Son had thought that the forsakenness was permanent rather than limited to His work of atonement, He would not have committed His spirit into the Father's hands. At this point, there must have been an understanding between Father and Son to make this final commitment meaningful.

Also, once the sacrifice was made and was acceptable to the Father, the normal pattern of Roman execution was interrupted. Instead of the victim's bones being broken to hasten his demise, Jesus's body was left intact so that the Old Testament prophecy would be fulfilled:

> Therefore, because it was the Preparation Day, that the bodies should not remain on the cross on the Sabbath (for that Sabbath was a high day), the Jews asked Pilate that their legs might be broken, and that they might be taken away. Then the soldiers came and broke the legs of the first and of the other who was crucified with Him. But when they came to Jesus and saw that He was already dead, they did not break His legs. But one of the soldiers pierced His side with a spear, and immediately blood and water came out. And he who has seen has testified, and his testimony is true; and he knows that he is telling the truth, so that you may believe. For these things were done that the Scripture should be fulfilled, "Not one of His bones shall be broken." And again another Scripture says, "They shall look on Him whom they pierced." (John 19:31–37)

In his sermon on the day of Pentecost, Peter proclaimed that the body of Jesus did not see corruption:

> Men and brethren, let me speak freely to you of the patriarch David, that he is both dead and buried, and his tomb is with us to this day. Therefore, being a prophet, and knowing that God had sworn with an oath to him that of the fruit of his body, according to the flesh, He would raise up the Christ to sit on his throne, he, foreseeing this, spoke concerning the resurrection of the Christ, that His soul was not left in Hades, nor did His flesh see corruption. This Jesus God has raised up, of which we are all witnesses. Therefore being exalted to the right hand of God, and having received from the Father the promise of the Holy Spirit, He poured out this which you now see and hear. (Acts 2:29–33)

Not only were the bones of Jesus left unbroken, but His body was not thrown into Gehenna, the garbage dump outside of Jerusalem. This dump, which had a continual fire to burn refuse, was used as a graphic image for hell. The custom of the Romans was to throw the bodies of executed criminals into this refuse heap to be consumed by flames. But Joseph of Arimathea, a wealthy man, asked Pilate for the corpse of Jesus so that He might be given a proper Jewish burial. The body of Jesus was then bound in strips of linen and placed in the garden tomb, in fulfillment of another Old Testament prophecy: "And they made His grave with the wicked—but with the rich at His death, because He had done no violence, nor was any deceit in His mouth" (Isa. 53:9).

All these details of the crucifixion and burial make it clear that the forsakenness Christ experienced was temporary. However, the ultimate evidence was the resurrection. The resurrection signified that the Father accepted the sacrifice of the Son. The fellowship of Christ with the Father was fully restored, vindicating the trust Jesus expressed in His final breath on the cross. The loyalty between the Father and the Son remained intact. In the process, God demonstrated His transcendent loyalty and love for the redeemed.

CHAPTER 4

THE LOVING-KINDNESS OF GOD

In our examination of the loyal love of God, we looked chiefly at
the opposite of loyalty—forsakenness. In this chapter, we will look
more directly at the positive side of this loyal love. One of the most
important words in the Old Testament is the Hebrew word *hesed*.
This word can be translated in various ways. Sometimes it refers to
God's mercy, sometimes to His covenantal steadfast love, sometimes
to His loving-kindness, and sometimes to His loyalty.

In the book of Micah, the question of God's requirements for His
people is raised. In a sense, the complex matter of obedience is reduced
to, or summarized by, three essential matters: "He has shown you, O
man, what is good; and what does the LORD require of you but to do
justly, to love mercy, and to walk humbly with your God?" (6:8).

The three virtues God requires are doing what is just, loving mercy, and walking in a spirit of humility before God. What we are most concerned with here is the second virtue, "to love mercy," which is a translation of *hesed*. The summary requirement that includes the obligation of showing this kind of love comes after a statement from God. The framework in which this threefold requirement is given is something like a legal trial.

One of the roles of the Old Testament prophets was to act as God's prosecuting attorneys when He brought suit against His people for breaking the terms of their covenant. The prophets announced God's covenant lawsuits against the people. We see the language of such a suit in the beginning of chapter 6: "Hear now what the LORD says: 'Arise, plead your case before the mountains, and let the hills hear your voice. Hear, O you mountains, the LORD's complaint, and you strong foundations of the earth; for the LORD has a complaint against His people, and He will contend with Israel. "O My people, what have I done to you? And how have I wearied you? Testify against Me"'" (vv. 1–3).

God called on the hills and the mountains to be witnesses to His complaint against Israel. He called on Israel to testify against Him, to indicate some justifiable reason for their infidelity to Him. God answered His own question by rehearsing the acts of redemption He had accomplished in behalf of Israel, harkening back to the exodus and reciting subsequent acts of His deliverance of them. The call to meet the obligations of the three virtues was a call for Israel to return to a state of fidelity to God and to the covenant with Him.

The call to *hesed* was a call to Israel to mirror and reflect the character of God Himself. He is the Author of loyal love, a love of mercy and kindness. Since He had shown His people this kind of love, He now commanded them to display this same kind of love in their dealings with one another.

The twin virtues of justice and mercy are to define the mutual relationships among people, as well as Israel's relationship with God. This love has been defined in hymnody as a love that "will not let me go" (from the hymn "O Love That Will Not Let Me Go," by George Matheson). It is a love that is never fickle but remains constant. It is an abiding love that is not abandoned at the first sign of strain. It is persistent and persevering, overcoming the irritations and annoyances that would threaten its continuity. It is a love that exhibits a vital bonding. In our day, the concept of "bonding" has been cheapened by overuse. In the classical sense, bonding involved a relationship that was so close it was as if the two parties were tied together with ropes. The cords were so tight that no amount of wiggling could allow either partner to squirm free. To be bonded can also suggest the metaphor of glue or cement that effects an adherence that withstands efforts to pry two objects apart or to break the seal between them.

The love that is called for here anticipates the summary of Jesus in the New Testament's Golden Rule. To do unto others as we would have them do unto us is to give others the kind of love that we would like to receive from them. The loyal love of *hesed* is both a duty and an opportunity. It is a duty in that it comes to us as a divine requirement or obligation. The duty makes love not simply a matter of feeling or emotion but an ethical matter that is rooted not in abstract philosophy but in theology and religious affection. At the same time, it offers an opportunity to experience the sweetness and excellency that flow from such a love.

The summary of Micah says that we are to do justice because God Himself is just. The Old Testament concept of justice is not an Aristotelian abstraction but is grounded in the character of God. To do justice is to do what is right. In the Old Testament, justice is always linked to righteousness. The two cannot be severed. To fail to do what is just is to act in an unrighteous manner. Likewise, to be unrighteous is to commit an injustice.

The justice that is required is not the rendering of a judge's verdict in a courtroom trial. The justice here is to be tempered by mercy. It is not punitive but is an expression of loving-kindness. It shows compassion. It is not only an act of mercy but actions that flow out of a love of mercy. The quality of *hesed* includes a delight in being merciful, not a stingy reluctance to show mercy.

The third virtue of walking humbly with God ties the justice and mercy to a personal relationship with God. The idea of walking with God is a strand that is woven throughout the tapestry of the Bible. The Old Testament saints were said to have "walked with God." In the New Testament, the Christian life is described in terms of walking along a certain path and in a certain manner. Before Christians were called "Christians" at Antioch (a term of derision), they were first called people of "the Way" (Acts 9:2; 11:26).

This manner of walking with God is enjoined in the first psalm: "Blessed is the man who walks not in the counsel of the ungodly, nor stands in the path of sinners, nor sits in the seat of the scornful; but his delight is in the law of the LORD, and in His law he meditates day and night" (vv. 1–2). The psalmist first stated his case for the blessed man in the negative. That is, he said what the blessed man does not do. He does not walk in the counsel of the ungodly. He avoids the path of sinners and refuses to occupy the chair of the cynic. Rather, his walk is a walk with God evidenced by a delight in His law and a meditation in it day and night.

HESED IN THE PROPHET HOSEA

There is no book of the Bible in which the Hebrew concept of *hesed* is more central and prominent than the book of Hosea. Since Hosea is known as the prophet of love in the Old Testament, he has often been called "the prophet of *hesed*." The issue of this kind of covenantal love is central to the book.

Micah functioned as a prosecuting attorney in a covenant lawsuit, and God used Hosea in a similar fashion. The complaint against His people is registered in chapter 4: "Hear the word of the LORD, you children of Israel, for the LORD brings a charge against the inhabitants of the land: 'There is no truth or mercy or knowledge of God in the land'" (v. 1).

The call to hear the word of the Lord is not an invitation to a fireside chat with Yahweh. Rather, it is a divine summons to a tribunal in which God will issue an indictment against His people. God Himself brings charges against Israel. The chief complaint concerns three matters: truth, mercy, and knowledge of God. All of these are said to be absent in the land.

Imagine a land where truth had vanished. In its place would be falsehood or sheer relativity.

The mercy that is absent is *hesed*. This mercy or loving-kindness had been transient, as seen by Hosea's comment in chapter 6: "O

Ephraim, what shall I do to you? O Judah, what shall I do to you? For your faithfulness is like a morning cloud, and like the early dew it goes away. Therefore I have hewn them by the prophets, I have slain them by the words of My mouth; and your judgments are like light that goes forth. For I desire mercy and not sacrifice, and the knowledge of God more than burnt offerings" (vv. 4–6)

The lack of faithfulness Hosea mentioned here is the absence of the fidelity or loyalty of *hesed*. It is like the dew that appears on the grass in the morning and quickly vanishes beneath the warmth of the sun. It is likened to a morning cloud that produces no rain. The cultic rituals performed by the people were empty and hypocritical. They were no substitute for the mercy and knowledge of God that He desired.

In the charge of chapter 4, not only are truth and loving-kindness missing, but also the knowledge of God. It is significant that the land being described as theologically ignorant is not Egypt or Babylonia. It is Israel, the land of the people to whom were entrusted the very oracles of God. This was the supremely blessed nation on whom God had poured out His special revelation of Himself. But now Israel was a barren landscape, a desert with respect to knowledge of the things of God.

Because of the absence of these things, the land was cast into mourning. Lying, theft, adultery, murder, and violence became commonplace. The indictment of chapter 4 continues:

> Now let no man contend, or rebuke another;
> For your people are like those who contend with the priest.
> Therefore you shall stumble in the day;

The prophet also shall stumble with you in the night;

And I will destroy your mother.

My people are destroyed for lack of knowledge.

Because you have rejected knowledge,

I also will reject you from being priest for Me;

Because you have forgotten the law of your God,

I also will forget your children. (vv. 4–6)

The grim consequence of the disappearance of the knowledge of God from the land was that the people began to perish. They were being destroyed. God's judgment was a judgment in kind, a poetic form of justice by which He declared that because His people had rejected Him, He would reject them from being priests for Him.

The Old Testament concept of apostasy was linked to forgetting. To forsake God was to forget Him and the benefits He had given to His people. Because the people forgot the law of God, He said that He would forget their children.

As we examine the concept of God's love in this prophetic book of love, we must keep in mind the situation in the land described in the indictment. It is against this backdrop that we must understand the earlier chapters of the book.

HOSEA AND GOMER

The episode of Hosea's marriage to Gomer has provoked much debate and controversy. Some have argued that the story is mere poetry and has no basis in historical fact. They view it as an illustrative allegory.

Some say that Gomer was not a prostitute at the time Hosea married her but fell into that role later. Some also suggest that the prostitution she engaged in was of a religious sort, the type found in cultic prostitution.

However, there is no reason not to take the story at face value. The historical reality may serve as an allegory in its application without consigning the actual event to the level of myth or legend. The story begins with an astonishing command from God:

> The word of the LORD that came to Hosea the son of Beeri, in the days of Uzziah, Jotham, Ahaz, and Hezekiah, kings of Judah, and in the days of Jeroboam the son of Joash, king of Israel.
>
> When the LORD began to speak by Hosea, the LORD said to Hosea:
> "Go, take yourself a wife of harlotry
> And children of harlotry,
> For the land has committed great harlotry
> By departing from the LORD." (1:1–2)

God's call for Hosea to marry a harlot was based on the spiritual adultery God's people had committed against Him. Just as forsakenness expresses the opposite of loyalty, adultery is the opposite of *hesed*. Here we see the value of defining concepts not only by what they mean positively but by what they exclude. There is always an antithesis to truth, that which contradicts or negates the truth. The antithesis of *hesed* is adultery or harlotry. This harlotry was also described in terms of a departure. Yahweh had not left His people.

Rather, God's people had departed from Him. This departure was likened to a spouse abandoning fidelity to the wedding vows. Such a departure indicates adultery.

Hosea obeyed the command of God and married Gomer. She then bore children to him, whose names carried symbolic significance. The firstborn child was a boy, who was given the name Jezreel: "So he went and took Gomer the daughter of Diblaim, and she conceived and bore him a son. Then the LORD said to him: 'Call his name Jezreel, for in a little while I will avenge the bloodshed of Jezreel on the house of Jehu, and bring an end to the kingdom of the house of Israel. It shall come to pass in that day that I will break the bow of Israel in the Valley of Jezreel'" (vv. 3–5).

This prophecy predicted the fall of the dynasty of Jeroboam II. The defeat would take place in the Valley of Jezreel. Jezreel had been the scene of bloody brutality exercised by Jehu, as recorded in 2 Kings 10:14.

The second child of Hosea and Gomer was a daughter, whom God commanded to be called Lo-Ruhamah: "And she conceived again and bore a daughter. Then God said to him: 'Call her name Lo-Ruhamah, for I will no longer have mercy on the house of Israel, but I will utterly take them away. Yet I will have mercy on the house of Judah, will save them by the LORD their God, and will not save them by bow, nor by sword or battle, by horses or horsemen'" (vv. 6–7).

The name Lo-Ruhamah means "the unpitied," or literally, "she has received no compassion." The meaning was clear for Israel. God would give Israel no more mercy. Israel would fall and go into exile. For years, God had shown compassion to Israel despite her constant violation of the covenant and her continual spiritual adultery. But God's patience had reached its limit, and He declared His judgment on her.

The third child of the union between Hosea and Gomer was a boy, who was to be called Lo-Ammi: "Now when she had weaned Lo-Ruhamah, she conceived and bore a son. Then God said: 'Call his name Lo-Ammi, for you are not My people, and I will not be your God. Yet the number of the children of Israel shall be as the sand of the sea, which cannot be measured or numbered. And it shall come to pass in the place where it was said to them, "You are not My people," there it shall be said to them, "You are sons of the living God"'" (vv. 8–10).

From henceforth the name of Israel was to be "Not My people." No greater tragedy can befall a nation than to change from being the people of God to not being the people of God. In this action, God announced that He would divorce Israel on the grounds of adultery.

Yet even here God tempered His justice with mercy by promising a future restoration of a remnant. The new Israel would also be numbered as the sand of the sea, according to the promise to Abraham and his descendants. Those who were to be called "Not My people" would then be called sons of the living God.

As God announced His divorce from Israel, so Hosea announced his divorce from Gomer:

> Bring charges against your mother, bring charges;
> For she is not My wife, nor am I her Husband!
> Let her put away her harlotries from her sight,
> And her adulteries from between her breasts;

Lest I strip her naked
And expose her, as in the day she was born,
And make her like a wilderness,
And set her like a dry land,
And slay her with thirst.

I will not have mercy on her children,
For they are the children of harlotry.
For their mother has played the harlot;
She who conceived them has behaved shamefully. (2:2–5)

Divorce, with the threat of exposure of her sins and the withdrawal of mercy from her children, was designed to be corrective and curative rather than punitive. Just as excommunication in the church has the goal of removing scandalous impurity from the church while leading the offender to penitence and to ultimate restoration to the church, so Hosea's divorce had a higher goal in mind. Hosea was trying to win back the affection of Gomer, as God would entice Israel:

"I will punish her
For the days of the Baals to which she burned incense.
She decked herself with her earrings and jewelry,
And went after her lovers;
But Me she forgot," says the LORD.

"Therefore, behold, I will allure her,
Will bring her into the wilderness,
And speak comfort to her.

I will give her her vineyards from there,
And the Valley of Achor as a door of hope;
She shall sing there,
As in the days of her youth,
As in the day when she came up from the land of Egypt."
(vv. 13–15)

Hosea pictured a blessed outcome for the future. He was confident that God would restore His bride to Himself despite her adultery. God promised to betroth Himself to His bride forever: "I will betroth you to Me forever; yes, I will betroth you to Me in righteousness and justice, in lovingkindness and mercy; I will betroth you to Me in faithfulness, and you shall know the LORD" (vv. 19–20). When God declared that He would betroth Israel to Himself in "faithfulness," the word He used was *hesed*.

Just as God promised to betroth Himself to an unfaithful bride, He commanded Hosea to do the same:

> Then the LORD said to me, "Go again, love a woman who is loved by a lover and is committing adultery, just like the love of the LORD for the children of Israel, who look to other gods and love the raisin cakes of the pagans."
>
> So I bought her for myself for fifteen shekels of silver, and one and one-half homers of barley. And I said to her, "You shall stay with me many days; you shall not play the harlot, nor shall you have a man—so, too, will I be toward you." (3:1–3)

It is noteworthy that in order for Hosea to get Gomer back as his wife he had to purchase her. He had to redeem her from her employers, who presumably were profiting from her prostitution. This purchase calls to mind the law of Exodus regarding indentured servants:

> Now these are the judgments which you shall set before them: If you buy a Hebrew servant, he shall serve six years; and in the seventh he shall go out free and pay nothing. If he comes in by himself, he shall go out by himself; if he comes in married, then his wife shall go out with him. If his master has given him a wife, and she has borne him sons or daughters, the wife and her children shall be her master's, and he shall go out by himself. (Exod. 21:1–4)

This passage is difficult for us to follow because it reflects an ancient custom with which we are not familiar. It states the law of God with respect to indentured servants. In antiquity, if a person was in such great debt that he was not able to pay his bills, he could exercise the option of becoming an indentured servant to the person he owed. The law required that when the term of labor expired, the servant was to be set free, along with his wife and children if he had brought them with him in the first place. However, if the servant took a wife from his master during the course of his servitude, then on his release he was not free to take his wife and children with him. Why? The answer lies in the concept of the bride-price that was to be paid by the male suitor to the father of the bride. Paying the price assured that the suitor had the necessary financial means to support and care for his wife.

When an indentured servant was set free, his debt was removed, but he was not financially independent. He still had no money to pay as a bride-price. Until he could secure such funds, he had to leave his wife and children with his former master, under the master's care and protection. For the husband and father to regain his wife and children, he had to redeem them by buying them back.

This elaborate system of redemption is frequently alluded to in the New Testament in describing how Christ redeems His people. He buys us out of slavery. We are therefore not our own but have been bought with a price (1 Cor. 6:20; 7:23). Just as Hosea had to purchase Gomer in order for their marriage to be restored, so Christ purchases us for Himself. He redeems His church by paying the bride-price for her.

After Hosea purchased Gomer, we learn nothing further of their life together. We hope that Gomer returned to him happily and remained faithful to their marriage for the rest of her days.

With respect to God's relationship to Israel, the rest of the book of Hosea enumerates many penalties that God would impose on her in His judgment. Yet the hope of future restoration remained intact: "How can I give you up, Ephraim? How can I hand you over, Israel? How can I make you like Admah? How can I set you like Zeboiim? My heart churns within Me; My sympathy is stirred. I will not execute the fierceness of My anger; I will not again destroy Ephraim. For I am God, and not man, the Holy One in your midst; and I will not come with terror" (11:8–9).

God rehearsed His past relationship with Israel, reminding her that when she was a child God loved her and called her out of Egypt. He reminded His people that He had taught them how to walk and had healed them from their wounds. Because of His love for them, God would not let them go. He gave them a final promise of restoration:

> I will heal their backsliding,
> I will love them freely,
> For My anger has turned away from him.
> I will be like the dew to Israel;
> He shall grow like the lily,
> And lengthen his roots like Lebanon.
> His branches shall spread;
> His beauty shall be like an olive tree,
> And his fragrance like Lebanon.
> Those who dwell under his shadow shall return;
> They shall be revived like grain,
> And grow like a vine.
> Their scent shall be like the wine of Lebanon.
>
> Ephraim shall say,
> "What have I to do anymore with idols?"
> I have heard and observed him.
> I am like a green cypress tree;
> Your fruit is found in Me. (14:4–8)

LOVING-KINDNESS

The concept of God's covenant love or mercy is found in the notion of His loving-kindness, an idea that figures prominently in the

Psalms. For example, in Psalm 17, a psalm of David, we hear David's call for it: "I have called upon You, for You will hear me, O God; incline Your ear to me, and hear my speech. Show Your marvelous lovingkindness by Your right hand, O You who save those who trust in You from those who rise up against them. Keep me as the apple of Your eye; hide me under the shadow of Your wings, from the wicked who oppress me, from my deadly enemies who surround me" (vv. 6–9).

David spoke of God's loving-kindness in terms of its marvelous character. He affirmed God's redeeming ways toward His people in protecting them from their enemies. David asked that he might be preserved as the "apple of God's eye," an expression of affection that persists to this day. God's protection of His beloved extends to the shelter of His wings, another common image in Hebrew poetry that likens God to a mother hen who protects her chicks from danger. It is the image used by Jesus in His lament over Jerusalem: "O Jerusalem, Jerusalem, the one who kills the prophets and stones those who are sent to her! How often I wanted to gather your children together, as a hen gathers her chicks under her wings, but you were not willing! See! Your house is left to you desolate; for I say to you, you shall see Me no more till you say, 'Blessed is He who comes in the name of the LORD!'" (Matt. 23:37–39).

We also see David's appeal to the loving-kindness of God in his classic psalm of penitence, Psalm 51: "Have mercy upon me, O God, according to Your lovingkindness; according to the multitude of Your tender mercies, blot out my transgressions. Wash me thoroughly from my iniquity, and cleanse me from my sin. For I acknowledge my transgressions, and my sin is always before me" (vv. 1–3).

In this penitential psalm, which was provoked by David's conviction of his sin with Bathsheba after Nathan the prophet confronted him, David pleaded with God that He not deal with him according to divine justice. David understood that if God were to deal with him according to His justice, he would perish. He acknowledged both his guilt and God's right to condemn him. But he begged God to deal with him according to His loving-kindness, which manifests itself in mercy. The mercy is further qualified by the adjective *tender*. There is a sweetness and gentleness to the mercy of God. This tender element defines the kindness of God's loving-kindness.

THE INSEPARABLE LOVE OF GOD

The constancy and loyalty of God's loving-kindness are displayed in its perseverance through all sorts of obstacles and trials. The ultimate expression of this loyal love is seen in Paul's teaching in Romans 8:

> What then shall we say to these things? If God is for us, who can be against us? He who did not spare His own Son, but delivered Him up for us all, how shall He not with Him also freely give us all things? Who shall bring a charge against God's elect? It is God who justifies. Who is he who condemns? It is Christ who died, and furthermore is also risen, who is even at the right hand of God, who also makes intercession for us. Who shall separate us from the love of Christ? Shall tribulation,

or distress, or persecution, or famine, or nakedness, or peril, or sword? As it is written:

"For Your sake we are killed all day long;
We are accounted as sheep for the slaughter."

Yet in all these things we are more than conquerors through Him who loved us. For I am persuaded that neither death nor life, nor angels nor principalities nor powers, nor things present nor things to come, nor height nor depth, nor any other created thing, shall be able to separate us from the love of God which is in Christ Jesus our Lord. (vv. 31–39)

In this passage, the Apostle set forth the principle that gripped the Reformers of the sixteenth century: *Deus pro nobis*, which means simply, "God for us." The source of Christian comfort is not that we are for God or that we are on His side. Rather, it is that God is for us and is on our side. To know that God is for us is to know that no one and nothing can ever prevail against us. Paul's question was clearly rhetorical: "If God is for us, who can be against us?" The answer is obvious: no one. Of course, this does not mean that Christians will have no enemies. On the contrary, we will be surrounded by enemies. Multitudes will set themselves against us. But these multitudinous enemies have no chance to destroy us because God has bound Himself to us. We are like Elisha at Dothan, surrounded by invisible angels who fight for us as the heavenly host (2 Kings 6:16–18).

What our enemies can never do, specifically, is separate us from the love of Christ. A "separation" is a kind of division. We see it often as a trial step in troubled marriages on the way to divorce.

Separation precedes the divorce and is often the harbinger of it. But in the marriage of Christ and His bride, there is neither divorce nor separation.

The "love of Christ" of which Paul spoke is not our love for Him but His love for us. Paul pointed to the risen and ascended Lord, who sits at the right hand of God and functions as our intercessor, our great High Priest. It is from His love and His care that we cannot be separated.

Paul listed specific things that threaten our security in this love. He spoke of tribulation, distress, persecution, famine, nakedness, peril, and sword. This list is by no means exhaustive, but it calls attention to several things that might cause us to faint or to doubt Christ's love for us. When we suffer persecution or the consequences of a famine, we may be inclined to fear that Christ has abandoned us. But Paul saw these perilous things as sufferings that accompany our discipleship to Christ. He quoted Psalm 44: "For Your sake we are killed all day long; we are accounted as sheep for the slaughter" (v. 22).

Even if we are subject to martyrdom, such suffering cannot cast asunder the love Christ has for us. In all these circumstances, there is victory because of the love of Christ.

Paul declared that in all these things we are "more than conquerors." The phrase "more than conquerors" translates a single word in Greek, which may be transliterated as *hypernikon.* The root of the word refers to the concept of conquest (such as is hinted by our Nike missiles or athletic shoes). The prefix *hyper* intensifies the root. Paul's point was that because of the love of Christ, we are not only conquerors in the face of all adversity, but we reach the supreme level of conquest, the zenith of victory in Him.

The Latin equivalent of the Greek *hypernikon* is the term *super-vincimus*. This indicates that in Christ we are not merely conquerors but superconquerors.

It is important to note that this apex of victory is achieved *through* Him. It is not achieved without Him or apart from Him. And the "Him" of whom Paul spoke here is defined and identified as "Him who loved us."

Paul then provided another list of things he was persuaded lack the power to separate us from the love of Christ. In this list are included death, life, angels, principalities, powers, things present, things to come, height, depth, and any other created thing. Once again the list Paul provided is not exhaustive but illustrative. He used hyperbole to communicate a truth. Not even the angels have the power to wrest us from the love of God in Christ. There is no clear and present danger, no future threat that has the power to divide us from Him. The forces of nature, the forces of government, the forces of hell—all lack the ability to sever us from Christ. In the face of the love of God in Christ, these creaturely powers are exposed as impotent.

In the next chapter, we will explore the relationship of God's love to His electing grace. In the meantime it is important to see that this inseparable love of which Paul spoke in Romans 8 is specifically directed to God's elect. It is the elect who enjoy the guarantee of this inseparable love. This discussion of the inseparable love of God in Christ takes place within the context of election. When Paul declared that God is for us, the "us" is defined as the elect. Paul asked rhetorically: "Who shall bring a charge against God's elect? It is God who justifies" (v. 33).

CHAPTER 5

THE ELECTING
LOVE OF GOD

The love of God, as we have seen, is rooted in His eternal covenant of redemption, His plan of salvation conceived before the foundation of the world. From all eternity, it was His plan to demonstrate His love through saving His elect.

The New Testament concept of election refers to God's act of choosing people to be recipients of His special grace or favor. It corresponds to the Old Testament concept of *bachar*, which refers to God's selective granting of His good pleasure. The concept of election is linked throughout Scripture with predestination.

We recognize that the idea of predestination, or divine election, is wrapped in controversy and is perilous to discuss. It brings us near to some of the deepest mysteries of God and touches on issues that provoke not only consternation but also often rage.

The idea of predestination was not conceived by Augustine, Martin Luther, or John Calvin. Though the doctrine of election figured prominently in the thought of these three giants of church history, it did not originate with them. The idea of predestination is rooted in the Bible. This is why all churches historically have found it necessary to formulate some doctrine of predestination in an effort to be biblical in their theology. The issue is not whether the Bible teaches the doctrine of predestination. The issue is which doctrine of predestination it teaches.

We encounter the doctrine of predestination in Paul's letter to the Ephesians:

> Blessed be the God and Father of our Lord Jesus Christ, who has blessed us with every spiritual blessing in the heavenly places in Christ, just as He chose us in Him before the foundation of the world, that we should be holy and without blame before Him in love, having predestined us to adoption as sons by Jesus Christ to Himself, according to the good pleasure of His will, to the praise of the glory of His grace, by which He made us accepted in the Beloved.
>
> In Him we have redemption through His blood, the forgiveness of sins, according to the riches of His grace which He made to abound toward us in all wisdom and prudence, having made known to us the mystery of His will, according to His good pleasure

which He purposed in Himself, that in the dispensation of the fullness of the times He might gather together in one all things in Christ, both which are in heaven and which are on earth—in Him. In Him also we have obtained an inheritance, being predestined according to the purpose of Him who works all things according to the counsel of His will, that we who first trusted in Christ should be to the praise of His glory.

In Him you also trusted, after you heard the word of truth, the gospel of your salvation; in whom also, having believed, you were sealed with the Holy Spirit of promise, who is the guarantee of our inheritance until the redemption of the purchased possession, to the praise of His glory. (1:3–14)

Here Paul began with a doxology in which he blessed God for having blessed us with spiritual blessings. These blessings are said to be "in Christ." The essence of these blessings in Christ is our election and all that goes with it. Indeed, the essence of the doctrine of election may be seen in these verses: "just as He chose us in Him before the foundation of the world, that we should be holy and without blame before Him in love, having predestined us to adoption as sons by Jesus Christ to Himself, according to the good pleasure of His will, to the praise of the glory of His grace, by which He made us accepted in the Beloved" (vv. 4–6).

Paul spoke here of God's having chosen us before the foundation of the world. He chose us that we should be holy and blameless in love. This choosing is then articulated in terms of God's having predestined us to adoption as sons. The basis of this election and predestination is "the good pleasure of His will."

ARBITRARY LOVE?

Paul did not ground election in the will of people but in the will of God. It is according to His good pleasure. Since election is not grounded in us, the question of the nature of God's will and of His love arises. Is His love arbitrary? That is, does He choose His elect in a whimsical or cavalier manner? Does He play dice with the salvation of His creatures?

In light of the biblical revelation of the character of God, it would seem that to ask such questions is to answer them. Nevertheless, the questions are raised repeatedly by those who struggle with divine election. It is important to see in this text that election and predestination are certainly according to the pleasure of God's will. But this pleasure of which Scripture speaks is not a sadistic or capricious pleasure. It is qualified by Scripture as the good pleasure of His will.

One would think that it would be unnecessary for the Holy Spirit to tell us that the pleasure of God's will is a good pleasure. The addition of the qualifying word *good* seems redundant. What kind of pleasure does God ever have except a good pleasure? Perhaps the Word of God supplies the qualifier simply to answer the objections of those who think the unthinkable, that God's love or God's will could ever really be arbitrary.

I think the problem arises when we consider that the basis of God's choice does not lie in us. We then leap to the conclusion that if the reason God chooses certain people and not others does not lie in them, He must make His choice for no reason at all. If His choice is for no reason, then it is both irrational and arbitrary.

But it is a gratuitous leap to assume that because the reason for our election is not in us, then there is no reason for it. Paul gave us a couple of hints here for the reasons behind divine election. The first is that it is to "the praise of the glory of His grace."

This is a crucial point. The purpose of God's election, in the first instance, is to the praise of His own glory. God is glorified when His love and mercy are displayed in election. Election shows His grace, and His grace displays His glory.

The second reason, which we will explore in more detail later, is that in His electing grace God made us accepted in the Beloved. There is no mystery as to the identity of the Beloved. "The Beloved" clearly refers to Christ. Our election is always in Christ. The first object of election is Christ Himself. He is the elect One from all eternity. The rest of the elect are elected in Him and for Him. The elect are the Father's gift to the Son.

Paul elaborated on this predestination in the very next passage:

> In Him we have redemption through His blood, the forgiveness of sins, according to the riches of His grace which He made to abound toward us in all wisdom and prudence, having made known to us the mystery of His will, according to His good pleasure which He purposed in Himself, that in the

dispensation of the fullness of the times He might gather together in one all things in Christ, both which are in heaven and which are on earth—in Him. In Him also we have obtained an inheritance, being predestined according to the purpose of Him who works all things according to the counsel of His will, that we who first trusted in Christ should be to the praise of His glory.

In Him you also trusted, after you heard the word of truth, the gospel of your salvation; in whom also, having believed, you were sealed with the Holy Spirit of promise, who is the guarantee of our inheritance until the redemption of the purchased possession, to the praise of His glory. (vv. 7–14)

We notice in this passage that election is a Trinitarian function. The Father elects and predestines, the election is in Christ, and the assurance of the fruits of election is wrought by the Holy Spirit. We are predestined "according to the purpose of Him who works all things according to the counsel of His will." This reveals that behind the electing love of God stands His sovereignty. We see that not only is God's will sovereign, but His love is sovereign.

DIVINE SOVEREIGNTY

When the issue of election and predestination arises, it is always attended with a discussion of the sovereignty of God. Rarely, if ever, does a professing Christian deny the thesis of the sovereignty of God. It is axiomatic to Christianity that God is sovereign. Manifestly, a God who is not sovereign is no God at all.

As facile as the confession of God's sovereignty is, putting substance to the confession is no easy matter at all. Indeed, when we begin to probe the content of sovereignty, we soon discover that the agreement we thought we had on the subject is at best tenuous. There are three major areas of concern with respect to God's sovereignty. First, He is sovereign in His authority over His creatures. Second, He is sovereign in His divine government over the universe and over history. Third, He is sovereign in the distribution of His saving grace.

At the theoretical level there is little dispute among Christians that God is sovereign in His right to rule over His creatures by His law. God has the right to impose obligations on us and to bind our consciences. That is, God has the sovereign right to rule over us and to declare "Thou shalt" or "Thou shalt not." While we usually agree with this aspect of divine sovereignty at the theoretical level, we reveal our disagreement at the practical level. Every time I sin I actually challenge God's right to rule over me. With every transgression against His law, I reject His sovereignty. Sin belies our true commitment to God's sovereign rule.

With respect to the second aspect of God's sovereignty, we also encounter serious disagreement among Christians. God's providential rule over the universe is in dispute. Classical theism affirms that God, in some sense, ordains whatever comes to pass. That is, He is sovereign in His government over every molecule in the universe and every event in history. He exercises this government in a mysterious way, without violating the wills of His creatures and without destroying secondary causes. He not only wills the ends by which His purposes come to pass, but also wills the means to those ends.

One of the most common ways God's sovereign government is denied is in the prevailing view of the laws of nature. Typically, the laws of nature (such as inertia or gravity) are described as if they were powers inherent in the material world that operate independently. That is, they are viewed as if they had primary causal power, the power to do things on their own, independent from any other agent. Such a view of nature is altogether pagan and incompatible with biblical Christianity.

The biblical worldview is that God is the source of all power. He alone has primary causality. He alone can work independently, without assistance from any other power. Scripture says that in Him "we live and move and have our being" (Acts 17:28). This means that without Him, or apart from Him, we could have no life, no motion, and no being. In fact, we do have life, we do move, and we do exist. We generate real power of motion, for example. At this moment, I am typing on a keyboard. God is not typing for me. I am moving my fingers according to my thoughts and my will. God is not coercing me to type what I type. But the exercise of power I am engaged in here is an example of secondary causality. As a secondary cause, I am exerting real power, but that power is always and everywhere dependent on the power of God for its potency.

Since all that happens in the universe ultimately depends on the power of God, ultimately God's sovereignty extends over all things. I choose to type what I type. God permits me to write these things, not necessarily because He sanctions them, but because even if I make errors, they may serve His will. The minute that I seek to type something God is not willing to have typed, He can and will stop me. He can thwart my efforts at any point. He has both the power and the right to stop me in my tracks at any moment. God is not obliged to let me do whatever I want to do lest He interfere with my free will. I have often heard the statement that God's sovereignty ends where man's freedom begins. Such a statement is not only false; it is blasphemous. If this were the case, then man and not God would be sovereign. This would be a pagan view of sovereignty.

Just the opposite is the case. Man is free, but God is also free. God's freedom is greater than man's. Man's freedom ends where God's sovereignty begins. It is God who works all things according to the counsel of His will. It is this assertion of the Apostle that chokes every humanist and stands as an immovable obstacle for every Pelagian.

When Paul said that God works all things according to the counsel of His will, we must remember that the God who is so working is the God of all of His attributes. His sovereign will is always His loving will.

The third aspect of God's sovereignty—the sovereignty of His distribution of grace—usually engenders the most controversy. God's sovereignty in this arena is frequently and vehemently challenged. That God has the right to be gracious to some and not to others becomes a matter of fierce debate. We see this in the context of Paul's teaching on the subject in Romans 9. We will address it as it arises in the broader context of his treatment of election there.

ROMANS 9

Paul began Romans 9 as follows:

> I tell the truth in Christ, I am not lying, my con-
> science also bearing me witness in the Holy Spirit,
> that I have great sorrow and continual grief in my
> heart. For I could wish that I myself were accursed
> from Christ for my brethren, my countrymen accord-
> ing to the flesh, who are Israelites, to whom pertain
> the adoption, the glory, the covenants, the giving
> of the law, the service of God, and the promises; of
> whom are the fathers and from whom, according to
> the flesh, Christ came, who is over all, the eternally
> blessed God. Amen. (vv. 1–5)

It is significant that Paul began this section of his epistle by
swearing an oath. The Apostle was clearly aware of the seriousness
of taking oaths and the danger of swearing such oaths in a frivolous
manner. Paul had been set apart by Christ to serve as the Apostle
to the Gentiles, but in this mission he never lost his zeal for his
own Hebrew people. Lest anyone should think that Paul had no
zeal for his kinsmen according to the flesh, he swore this solemn
oath here. He spoke of his grief for his own people and even went
so far as to declare that he would be willing to be cursed himself if
such cursing would ensure the redemption of his people. He stated
categorically that he was willing to trade his own redemption for
theirs.

Paul then quickly pointed out that despite the grim state of affairs for Israel, particularly after their rejection of the Messiah, this historical turn of events did not negate God's eternal plan of salvation:

> But it is not that the word of God has taken no effect. For they are not all Israel who are of Israel, nor are they all children because they are the seed of Abraham; but, "In Isaac your seed shall be called." That is, those who are the children of the flesh, these are not the children of God; but the children of the promise are counted as the seed. For this is the word of promise: "At this time I will come and Sarah shall have a son."
>
> And not only this, but when Rebecca also had conceived by one man, even by our father Isaac (for the children not yet being born, nor having done any good or evil, that the purpose of God according to election might stand, not of works but of Him who calls), it was said to her, "The older shall serve the younger." As it is written, "Jacob I have loved, but Esau I have hated." (vv. 6–13)

Perhaps this passage more than any other in the Bible clearly sets forth the idea of divine election and predestination. This text has been tortured by those who find the biblical doctrine of predestination repugnant. Because of its singular importance, we will look more closely at some of its elements.

First of all, we see Paul affirm that Israel's disobedience did not negate God's plan of salvation, because "they are not all Israel who are of Israel." This is a critical point because the Apostle distinguished between the whole group of people who are subsumed under the class "Israel" and the smaller portion within the larger group, which the Bible frequently refers to as the "remnant" of Israel. Neither, the Apostle said, are all of the descendants of Abraham the children of God's covenant promise to Abraham. He reminded his readers that Ishmael was the son of Abraham, but he was not the child of promise. Already, in the offspring of Abraham, the function of divine election was at work. Isaac was chosen in a manner that Ishmael clearly was not.

Paul labored the point that the Pharisees so often missed, namely, that election does not proceed by biological or ethnic inheritance. It is not the children of the flesh who are elect but the children of the promise. This was seen most clearly and most dramatically in God's election of Jacob over Esau. This selection by God indicates several things. First of all, we see that not all of the seed of Isaac are elect. Just as God distinguished between the sons of Abraham, Ishmael and Isaac, He distinguished between Jacob and Esau. In the case of Jacob and Esau, it was not a matter of who was the mother, for they had the same mother, Rebecca. The two were fully brothers, and not only were they brothers, they were twin brothers.

Second, we see that the normal order of inheritance was reversed. The custom was for the elder son to receive the patriarchal blessing and the lion's share of the inheritance. However, Jacob received the blessing, even though Esau was the firstborn. How that worked out in history was a matter of chicanery and deceit. Nevertheless, the divine decree predated the historical struggle between the brothers.

One of the common objections to the doctrine of election Paul taught here is the thesis that Paul was not talking about the election of individuals to receive special grace from God but the election of nations. Jacob became the father of Israel, so redemptive history followed the course of his family and not Esau's. The problem with this explanation is that it collides violently with the text. Even if Paul were speaking of national destinies and not personal destinies, he chose to argue his point not by speaking of nations but of specific individuals, Jacob and Esau.

THE PRESCIENT VIEW OF ELECTION

The most common alternative to the Reformation understanding of this text is called the prescient view of election. This view is based on a particular understanding of the relationship between God's foreknowledge and His election. In this schema, God peers down through the corridors of time and sees in advance what the future decisions of people will be. Those whom He sees will choose Christ, He elects unto salvation. Those whom He sees will reject Christ, He rejects.

In this scenario, the decisive factor in election is the choice of the sinners who correctly respond to God's offer of grace. The decision of God rests on His foreknowledge of the decisions of men. It is man's free will that determines his election or nonelection.

This view of election suffers from several fatal flaws. Among them is that the view flatly contradicts the very point Paul made in Romans 9. What did he mean by writing "(for the children not yet being born, nor having done any good or evil, that the purpose of God according to election might stand, not of works but of Him who calls)"? Obviously the prescient view of election has God doing His electing before Jacob and Esau were born, as does virtually every view of election. But the prescient view is based on Jacob and Esau doing good or evil. If Paul was teaching the prescient view here, why did he point out that the election occurred *before* the children had done any good or evil? If he was concerned only with the time frame of their election, this clause is superfluous. At this point, the prescient view begs the question. Paul's point was manifestly that election is not based on any activity, any work, or (as we will see later) any choice of man. Paul set the grounds of election not in the will of man but in the will of God so that God's purpose of election might stand. It is the will of God, not the will of man, that is decisive.

The other severe problem faced by advocates of the prescient view is that it ignores the fallen condition of man, which has left him in a state of moral inability, as taught by Jesus. In the gospel of John, we read:

> Therefore many of His disciples, when they heard this, said, "This is a hard saying; who can understand it?"
>
> When Jesus knew in Himself that His disciples complained about this, He said to them, "Does this offend you? What then if you should see the Son of Man ascend where He was before? It is the Spirit who gives life; the flesh profits nothing. The words that I speak to you are spirit, and they are life. But there are some of you who do not believe." For Jesus

knew from the beginning who they were who did not believe, and who would betray Him. And He said, "Therefore I have said to you that no one can come to Me unless it has been granted to him by My Father."

From that time many of His disciples went back and walked with Him no more. Then Jesus said to the twelve, "Do you also want to go away?"

But Simon Peter answered Him, "Lord, to whom shall we go? You have the words of eternal life." (6:60–68)

In the first instance, Jesus taught that the flesh of fallen humanity profits nothing. This was why He had instructed Nicodemus that it was necessary for a person to be born again to see the kingdom of God (John 3:3). He said that what was born of the flesh is flesh. In order to see the kingdom, one must be born of the Spirit. Here in chapter 6, Jesus reaffirmed this truth that the flesh does not profit. But those who hold to the prescient view have people who are not regenerate choosing Christ, securing their own election, and thus profiting everything. They may grant that mankind is weakened by the fall but not to such a degree that people must be born again before they can exercise faith. Instead, they teach that first one must have faith and then one will be reborn. This is the exact opposite of the biblical order, in which regeneration or rebirth must *precede* faith. This regeneration then yields not only the possibility of faith but also its very reality.

Jesus said, "No one can come to Me unless it has been granted to him by My Father." If we analyze this, we see that "no one" indicates a universal negative proposition. It means that none in a certain class have the predicate attributed to them. What is being described in terms of a universal negative? Jesus said, "No one can." Jesus was speaking here of power or ability to do something. Since He spoke of this particular ability in universal negative terms, He was describing a universal inability. This inability is specified. It is an inability to "come to Me." In what sense was Jesus speaking about coming to Him? Surely He was not speaking of a person's physical inability to approach Him on the street. Many people approached Him physically, both friends and enemies. The language of "coming" to Jesus is elliptical here and can only mean coming to Him in faith. It is that kind of coming that no one can do unless the Father does something first. Jesus said that no one could come to Him "unless." A necessary condition must be met before a desired result can follow. The necessary condition in view here is the gift of God.

In this passage, Jesus reiterated what He said a little earlier: "Do not murmur among yourselves. No one can come to Me unless the Father who sent Me draws him; and I will raise him up at the last day" (6:43–44).

Here Jesus used the same universal negative, but He cited the necessary condition that must be met for anyone to come to Him: the Father must *draw* that person. This word has often been emptied of its full force and reduced to a kind of divine wooing, enticing, or attracting, which people can and do resist. However, the word that is translated "draw" here is translated "drag" elsewhere in the New Testament and is defined in the most authoritative Greek dictionary to mean "compel."

The reaction of those who heard Jesus twice proclaim the moral inability of people to come to Him without divine intervention is interesting. After this hard saying, many of Jesus's disciples left Him and walked with Him no more. He asked those who remained if they also would go away, to which Peter replied: "Lord, to whom shall we go? You have the words of eternal life" (v. 68). We wonder why anyone would have been offended by Jesus's words if He were teaching the prescient view of election or was articulating a semi-Pelagian view of the fall, which claims that though man requires grace from God to be saved, in the final analysis that grace can be accepted or rejected. This soft view of election brings little if any offense. It is not the kind of teaching that would provoke many of Jesus's disciples to walk away from Him. However, this is frequently people's response when they encounter the Reformation understanding and teaching of election.

Another response to Romans 9 is the widespread rejection of the notion of double predestination. Some argue that predestination is true only in the positive sense. That is, although some people are elected to salvation, no one is rejected by God's eternal decree. This runs against what Paul says about Jacob and Esau. Jacob received something that Esau did not receive. Unless God elects all people to salvation, which this text clearly rejects, then some people are in the category of the nonelect, or the reprobate. One cannot speak of particular election without facing that at the same time some do not receive this supreme benefit of grace. If we are to avoid universalism, then the election of some can only mean the nonelection of others.

There is confusion about double predestination. Some conceive it to mean that God works in the same way in the hearts of the reprobate as He does in the hearts of the elect. This involves a symmetrical view of election or a view of "equal ultimacy." This view would mean that just as God works faith in the hearts of the elect, so He works unbelief in the hearts of the reprobate. This is not the Reformation view of double predestination. In the Reformation view, God considers the human race in its fallenness. Out of this mass of fallen humanity, He chooses to save some while passing over others. He is active with respect to the elect but passive with respect to the reprobate. The elect receive God's saving grace. The reprobate receive God's justice. No one receives injustice, which I will explore further later.

In Romans 9, we see clearly that predestination is double because Esau did not receive the positive benefit that was conferred on Jacob. The difference between the two is expressed in terms of divine love and divine hatred. Surely the most difficult part of this text is not found in the words "Jacob have I loved," but in the words "Esau have I hated." This expression is so jarring and so subject to serious misunderstanding that, once again, I will defer its treatment to a later chapter.

In the meantime, let us proceed to the next portion of Romans 9:

> What shall we say then? Is there unrighteousness with
> God? Certainly not! For He says to Moses, "I will have
> mercy on whomever I will have mercy, and I will have
> compassion on whomever I will have compassion." So
> then it is not of him who wills, nor of him who runs,
> but of God who shows mercy. For the Scripture says
> to the Pharaoh, "For this very purpose I have raised
> you up, that I may show My power in you, and that

My name may be declared in all the earth." Therefore
He has mercy on whom He wills, and whom He wills
He hardens. (vv. 14–18)

It is significant that immediately after declaring his view of the election of Jacob and the rejection of Esau, Paul raised a rhetorical question. The Apostle often used this device in setting forth an argument. With the rhetorical question, he anticipated an objection from his reader. Note carefully what objection he anticipated. He asked, "What shall we say then? Is there unrighteousness with God?"

I wonder whether any advocate of the prescient view of election has ever had to respond to this objection. In that view, there would be no reason for anyone to protest God's being unrighteous. It places the deciding factor of election not on God's sovereign distribution of His saving grace but on the human choice to receive that grace. It would seem perfectly just and righteous for God to reject someone who first rejects His grace.

That Paul included this rhetorical question here and anticipated a protest concerning God's righteousness gives me great comfort in my understanding of this text. I say that because every advocate of the Reformation understanding of election is constantly faced with the charge that it makes God unrighteous.

IS ELECTION UNFAIR?

The teaching that God chooses some people out of the mass of fallen humanity to be saved and not others raises the objection that God is not fair. Somehow it is widely assumed that God owes all people either the gift of salvation or at least a chance of salvation. Since they cannot be saved apart from His grace, He owes it to everyone to grant them that grace.

This kind of thinking results from a fundamental confusion between God's justice and His mercy or grace. Grace, by definition, is something that God is not required to grant. He owes a fallen world no mercy. If we cried out for justice at His hands, we could all receive the just condemnation we deserve. Justice is what we deserve. Grace is always and ever undeserved. If we deserved it, it would not be grace.

The issue is complicated when we consider that God chooses to grant this saving grace to some but not to all. We recall that, in the first place, He owes it to no one. Once someone has sinned, God owes that person nothing. Indeed, even before sin, God owes the creature nothing. It is the creature who is indebted to God (for sustaining if not also saving grace), not God to the creature. But what is often assumed is that if God grants grace to some, then He must grant the same measure of grace to all if He is fair and just. Here we must stop for a moment and ask why this should be so. Why does the granting of grace to some require the granting of grace to all? Again we recall that in this process no one receives injustice at the hand of God. The elect get the grace they do not deserve, while the reprobate get the justice they do deserve. If God decides to pardon one guilty person, that does not mean that those He does not pardon somehow become any less guilty.

In answer to his own question, "Is there unrighteousness with God?" Paul emphatically declared, "Certainly not!" For the

Apostle, it was unthinkable that there should be any unrighteousness with God. He reminded his readers of what God revealed in the Old Testament when He said to Moses, "I will be gracious to whom I will be gracious, and I will have compassion on whom I will have compassion" (Exod. 33:19).

We see in this reminder the unmistakable concept of God's sovereign grace. Paul made it unambiguously clear that God always reserves the right to exercise His mercy and grace according to His own good pleasure. This is the supreme right of executive clemency. It is this sovereign expression of love that redounds to the praise of His glory. It is this love that leaves us astonished and singing doxologies. It is this overwhelming love that provoked Paul to cry out: "Oh, the depth of the riches both of the wisdom and knowledge of God! How unsearchable are His judgments and His ways past finding out! 'For who has known the mind of the LORD? Or who has become His counselor?' 'Or who has first given to Him and it shall be repaid to him?'" (Rom. 11:33–35).

The conclusion Paul drew from this sovereign expression of grace and mercy is this: "So then it is not of him who wills, nor of him who runs, but of God who shows mercy" (9:16). In light of the plain sense of these words, it is astounding that the prescient view of election persists so widely. The prescient view clearly does not set forth the biblical view of election; it flatly denies it. In this view, in the final analysis, the cause of salvation is grounded in the one who wills or the one who runs, not in God, who shows mercy. But the Bible tells us that God in His sovereignty bestows His saving grace freely and effectively on whom He wills, and brings them to Christ and to Himself.

Perhaps the greatest expression of God's love in the Reformed schema is His granting to His elect the very requirement He makes of men to avail the benefits of Christ. It is the granting of the gift of faith. Here the Holy Spirit ensures the efficacy of the work of the Son by quickening some from spiritual death unto spiritual life and giving the gift of faith. Paul made this clear in Ephesians 2:

> And you He made alive, who were dead in trespasses and sins, in which you once walked according to the course of this world, according to the prince of the power of the air, the spirit who now works in the sons of disobedience, among whom also we all once conducted ourselves in the lusts of our flesh, fulfilling the desires of the flesh and of the mind, and were by nature children of wrath, just as the others.
>
> But God, who is rich in mercy, because of His great love with which He loved us, even when we were dead in trespasses, made us alive together with Christ (by grace you have been saved), and raised us up together, and made us sit together in the heavenly places in Christ Jesus, that in the ages to come He might show the exceeding riches of His grace in His kindness toward us in Christ Jesus. For by grace you have been saved through faith, and that not of yourselves; it is the gift of God, not of works, lest anyone should boast. For we are His workmanship, created in Christ Jesus for good works, which God prepared beforehand that we should walk in them. (vv. 1–10)

The electing love of God is in view here with respect to His graciousness in quickening us from death to life, not after we responded to the gospel, but in order that we could and would respond to the gospel. He said that we are saved by grace through faith, and that not of ourselves; it is the gift of God. What then is this gift? Is it grace or faith? In this text, the antecedent of "that" is faith, so that the sovereign love of God is expressed in the sovereign grace of God in granting to the elect the gift of faith by which they receive the benefits of Christ.

CHAPTER 6

LOVE AND HATE
IN GOD

It is one thing for us to consider the depths and riches of the love of God. We have seen that He is so loving in His character that the Bible can say He *is* love. But it is quite another matter for us to contemplate the hatred of God. Hatred—at least hatred directed at people—seems to be totally antithetical to the character of God. We may be comfortable with the adage that God hates the sin but loves the sinner but find it completely unimaginable that God could hate both the sin *and* the sinner.

In Romans 9, Paul spoke not only of God's love for Jacob but also of His hatred for Esau: "And not only this, but when Rebecca also had conceived by one man, even by our father Isaac (for the children not yet being born, nor having done any good or evil, that the purpose of God according to election might stand, not of works but of Him who calls), it was said to her, 'The older shall serve the younger.' As it is written, 'Jacob I have loved, but Esau I have hated'" (vv. 10–13).

How are we to understand this reference to God's hatred for Esau? Are we not taught with regularity that God loves everyone? If He does love everyone, it would not be possible for Him to hate anyone. Conversely, if it is true that He hates anyone, He could not at the same time love everyone. This is so because love and hate are incompatible opposites.

In chapter 7, when we examine the distinctive types of the love of God, I will try to show that certain types of God's love can coexist with a type of divine hatred. In the meantime, however, we can say that God may love a person in one sense or in one way while at the same time hating him in another sense or another way. In essence, not all kinds of divine love are absolutely antithetical to all kinds of divine hatred.

We understand this distinction at least intuitively when we affirm the love of God on the one hand and the punitive wrath of God on the other hand. We know, for example, that the Bible teaches that God sends people to hell. We may find relief by saying that God hates the sin but loves the sinner. But that relief is jolted by the reality that it is not the sin God sends to hell; it is the sinner.

How, then, are we to understand the biblical references to the hatred of God? Many commentators treat Paul's declaration of God's hatred for Esau as merely a "manner of speaking." We remember that Paul's statement in Romans 9 is actually a quote from the Old Testament book of Malachi. The full quote reads:

The burden of the word of the LORD to Israel by
Malachi.

"I have loved you," says the LORD.
"Yet you say, 'In what way have You loved us?'
Was not Esau Jacob's brother?"
Says the LORD.
"Yet Jacob I have loved;
But Esau I have hated,
And laid waste his mountains and his heritage
For the jackals of the wilderness."

Even though Edom has said,
"We have been impoverished,
But we will return and build the desolate places." (1:1–4)

It is possible that both in Malachi and in Romans the reference
to God's hatred for Esau may reflect a Hebrew idiom that simply
communicates a preference. If I prefer chocolate ice cream to vanilla,
I might express that preference by saying, "I love chocolate and hate
vanilla." To the Jew, this would not mean that I loathed vanilla. In
fact, I might even like vanilla, but when confronted with the option
of vanilla or chocolate, my preference would be chocolate.

This idiom of preference may be seen in the Genesis account of
Jacob's wife Leah:

When the LORD saw that Leah was unloved, He opened
her womb; but Rachel was barren. So Leah conceived

and bore a son, and she called his name Reuben; for she said, "The LORD has surely looked on my affliction. Now therefore, my husband will love me." Then she conceived again and bore a son, and said, "Because the LORD has heard that I am unloved, He has therefore given me this son also." And she called his name Simeon. She conceived again and bore a son, and said, "Now this time my husband will become attached to me, because I have borne him three sons." (29:31–34)

In this text, Leah is described as "unloved." This is an example of the idiom of preference. That Leah was not literally unloved but was only relatively unloved in terms of preference is seen clearly from the text that immediately precedes the one just cited: "So he gave him his daughter Rachel as wife also. And Laban gave his maid Bilhah to his daughter Rachel as a maid. Then Jacob also went in to Rachel, and he also loved Rachel more than Leah. And he served with Laban still another seven years" (vv. 28–30).

Jacob loved Rachel more than he loved Leah. This does not mean that Leah was "unloved" by Jacob in a literal sense. Again, what is expressed is a preference.

We see a similar use of this Hebrew idiom in a New Testament text that has often baffled interpreters:

Now great multitudes went with Him. And He turned and said to them, "If anyone comes to Me and does not hate his father and mother, wife and children, brothers and sisters, yes, and his own life also, he cannot be My disciple. And whoever does not bear his cross and come after Me cannot be My disciple. For which of you, intending to build a tower, does not sit down first and count the cost, whether he has enough to finish it—lest, after he has laid the foundation, and is not able to finish, all who see it begin to mock him, saying, 'This man began to build and was not able to finish.' Or what king, going to make war against another king, does not sit down first and consider whether he is able with ten thousand to meet him who comes against him with twenty thousand? Or else, while the other is still a great way off, he sends a delegation and asks conditions of peace. So likewise, whoever of you does not forsake all that he has cannot be My disciple." (Luke 14:25–33)

Jesus established a criterion for discipleship that requires "hating" one's father and mother, spouse and children, brothers and sisters. If we were to take this passage literally, it would flatly contradict what Scripture elsewhere requires of us. The Bible teaches that we are to honor our parents, to love our wives, and so on. Yet, if I obey the Word of God and love my wife, then in light of Jesus's words here, it seems that I am disqualified from being His disciple. That is, unless we understand His requirement to "hate" our parents and others in terms of the Hebrew idiom of preference. Stated simply, Jesus was saying we must love Him above all others if we are to be His disciples. Here, the word *hate* clearly means "to love less."

Though understanding this idiom ameliorates the difficulty of understanding God's hatred of Esau, it does not solve the problem altogether. The text of Malachi, particularly, goes beyond the level of mere preference. It speaks of an active judgment of God against Esau. It describes God laying waste Esau's mountains and his inheritance. Here God's hatred includes His actual rejection of Esau. Esau is not only passed over as the blessing is given to Jacob; he is the object of divine justice and punishment.

Though the text suggests more by the term *hated* than mere preference, a link still remains between the literary device of idiom and the more severe understanding of hatred that includes divine judgment. One of the most common literary forms in Hebrew is parallelism, especially in Hebrew poetry. There are several types of parallelism. One of the most common is *antithetical parallelism*, in which the truth of a positive assertion is reinforced by expressing its negative form in close conjunction. We see this in Isaiah 45:

> I am the LORD, and there is no other;
> I form the light and create darkness,
> I make peace and create calamity;
> I, the LORD, do all these things. (vv. 6–7)

The contrast between light and darkness is clear in this passage. In the next couplet we see peace and calamity contrasted. As it is written here, this passage poses no problem for us. However, the older King James Version translates this text this way: "I make peace, and create evil." Because of this earlier rendition, people thought the Bible taught that God was the author of evil. The text plainly declared that God creates evil. But the evil that is in view is not moral evil; rather, it is the calamity that God in His providence brings about in times of judgment. Had the parallelism been detected by readers of the King James Version in past centuries, it would have been immediately clear that the text was not suggesting God is the author of sin.

If we have an example of antithetical parallelism in Romans 9, then we understand that the hatred of Esau is an expression of contrast to the love of Jacob. In this regard, all that is meant is that whereas Jacob received the supreme divine blessing, that blessing is withheld from Esau. The contrast in Romans 9 is between God's mercy and His justice. We remember that Paul reminded his readers that God reserves the right to have mercy on whom He will have mercy. It is obvious in this context that Jacob received a measure of God's mercy that Esau did not receive. In his election, Jacob received mercy and grace. In his rejection, Esau received justice and judgment.

But Malachi is not the only place where Scripture speaks of God's hatred for people. We see it also expressed, for example, in Psalm 5:

> For You are not a God who takes pleasure in wickedness,
> Nor shall evil dwell with You.
> The boastful shall not stand in Your sight;
> You hate all workers of iniquity.
> You shall destroy those who speak falsehood;
> The LORD abhors the bloodthirsty and deceitful man.
> (vv. 4–6)

The psalmist used strong language to express God's hostility toward the wicked. Not only did he declare that God hates all workers of iniquity, but he escalated the language of hatred to the level of abhorrence. To abhor something is to regard it with extreme distaste and even disgust. The term is used frequently in the Old Testament to express God's disdain for the hypocritical worship of His people. This abhorrence can be expressed with words such as *detest* or *despise*, as we see in Amos 5:

> I hate, I despise your feast days,
> And I do not savor your sacred assemblies.
> Though you offer Me burnt offerings and your grain
>   offerings,
> I will not accept them,
> Nor will I regard your fattened peace offerings.
> Take away from Me the noise of your songs,
> For I will not hear the melody of your stringed
>   instruments.
> But let justice run down like water,
> And righteousness like a mighty stream. (vv. 21–24)

I do not think it is an overstatement to say that the Bible speaks as much about God's hatred as it does about His love. We have a tendency to ignore the many references to God's abhorrence of sinners or to allow that detestation to be swallowed up in a broader sense of His love.

THE UNCONDITIONAL LOVE OF GOD

One manifestation of our focus on God's love is our willingness to declare to the world that God loves everyone unconditionally. In fact, it has become fashionable in evangelical circles to speak somewhat glibly of the unconditional love of God. It is certainly a pleasing message for people to hear and conforms to a certain kind of political correctness. In our desire to communicate to people the sweetness of the gospel, the readiness of God to cover our sins with forgiveness, and the incredible depth of His love displayed on the cross, we indulge in a hyperbolic expression of the scope and extent of His love.

Where in Scripture do we find this notion of the unconditional love of God? If God's love is absolutely unconditional, why do we tell people that they have to repent and have faith in order to be saved? God sets forth clear conditions for a person to be saved. It may be true that in some sense God loves even those who fail to meet the conditions of salvation, but that subtlety is often missed by the hearer when the preacher declares the unconditional love of God. People hear that God will continue to love them and accept them, no matter what they do or how they live. We might as well declare an unabashed universalism as to declare the unconditional love of God without a clear and careful qualification of what that means.

An interesting contrast can be seen by comparing the preaching of eighteenth- and nineteenth-century evangelists with modern evangelists. The stress in earlier centuries was on the wrath of God directed toward impenitent sinners. Indeed, Jonathan Edwards's preaching has been described as evangelistic preaching that employed a "scare theology." That approach has given way to a more positive emphasis on God's love. Of course, Edwards also declared the love of God, but not without reminding sinners that as long as they remained impenitent, they were exposed to the wrath of God and were in fact heaping up wrath against the day of wrath (Rom. 2:5).

Edwards warned his people that they were more repugnant to God in their sin than rebellious subjects were to their princes. This was part and parcel of proclaiming the gospel of reconciliation. There can be no talk of reconciliation without first establishing that there is some prior alienation or estrangement. Parties who are not estranged do not need reconciliation. The biblical concept of reconciliation presupposes a condition of estrangement between God and man.

Much is said of man's hostility toward God. The Bible says we are God's enemies by nature. This enmity is expressed in our sinful rebellion against Him. The common contemporary view of this is that we are estranged from God, but He is not estranged from us. The enmity is all one sided. The picture we get is that God goes on loving us with an unconditional love while we remain hateful toward Him.

The cross belies this picture. Yes, the cross occurred because God loves us. His love stands behind His plan of salvation. However, Christ was not sacrificed on the cross to placate us or to serve as a propitiation to us. His sacrifice was not designed to satisfy our unjust enmity toward God but to satisfy God's just wrath toward us. The Father was the object of the Son's act of propitiation. The effect of the cross was to remove the divine estrangement from us, not our estrangement from Him. If we deny God's estrangement from us, the cross is reduced to a pathetic and anemic moral influence with no substitutionary satisfaction of God.

In Christ, the obstacle of estrangement is overcome, and we are reconciled to God. But that reconciliation extends only to believers. Those who reject Christ remain at enmity with God, estranged from

God, and objects both of His wrath and of His abhorrence. Whatever kind of love God has for the impenitent, it does not exclude His just hatred and abhorrence of them, which stands in stark contrast to His redeeming love.

THE FORELOVE OF GOD

The way Scripture speaks of the foreknowledge of God communicates a certain foreloving of His elect. This is expressed in the "golden chain" of Romans 8: "And we know that all things work together for good to those who love God, to those who are the called according to His purpose. For whom He foreknew, He also predestined to be conformed to the image of His Son, that He might be the firstborn among many brethren. Moreover whom He predestined, these He also called; whom He called, these He also justified; and whom He justified, these He also glorified" (vv. 28–30).

Romans 8:28 is one of the most comforting texts in all of Scripture. It assures the believer that all "tragedies" are ultimately blessings. It does not declare that all things that happen are good in and of themselves, but that God is working in and through all the things that happen to us for our good. This is also firmly grounded in His eternal purpose for His people.

The next verse then speaks both of God's foreknowledge and of His predestination. This text is a favorite of those who advocate the prescient view of predestination. The inference drawn from this verse is that God's predestination is based on His foreknowledge of future events. Again, the idea is that God looks down the corridor of time and sees in advance how people will respond to the offer of the gospel. He then predestines to salvation those who will someday embrace the gospel. His election of them is based on their foreknown decision.

There are serious problems with this view. The first we have already considered, namely, that Paul explicitly teaches a few verses later that it is not in him who wills (Rom. 9:16). If the prescient view is correct, then it is precisely in him who wills. Beyond that consideration is the assumption that because God's foreknowledge is mentioned before His predestination, the predestination is therefore because of or based on that foreknowledge. This is a possible inference but by no means a necessary inference. To treat it as a necessary inference is to fall into the trap of the *post hoc* logical fallacy. Because one thing follows another does not prove that it was caused by the other. Because the rooster crows and then the sun rises does not mean that if we kill the rooster, the sun will not rise again.

Whether one assumes the prescient view of election or the Reformation view, it is necessary for foreknowledge to precede predestination. God could hardly predestine unknown people to salvation. Whomever He predestined He must have known; otherwise, He would not have been predestinating them. For God to have chosen Jacob from the foundation of the world, He had to have known Jacob from the foundation of the world. Therefore, it is not at all surprising that Paul, in teaching us about predestination and divine election, puts God's foreknowledge at the beginning of the chain.

In this chain, we are concerned with what is called in theology the "order of salvation" (*ordo salutis*). This order is not necessarily temporal or chronological but rather logical. For example, when we speak of the relationship between faith and justification, we say that justification is by faith, meaning that faith is a necessary condition for justification. One must have faith in order to be justified. In this sense, we say that faith "comes before" or precedes justification. But then we must ask the question, "How long must we have faith before we are justified?" The answer is clear—there is no time lapse between faith and justification. The moment we have true faith we have with it justification. In reality, faith and justification occur simultaneously. Why then do we speak of an order? Again, the answer is found in logical priority; we understand that justification depends on faith and not faith on justification.

The question of the order of salvation has been at the core of some of the most serious disputes in church history. For example, the issue between the Roman Catholic Church and the Reformers can be expressed in terms of the order between justification and sanctification. Does justification rest on sanctification, or does sanctification rest on justification? Likewise, the ongoing debate between Calvinism and Arminianism focuses on the order of regeneration and faith. Does one need to have faith in order to be regenerated, or does one need to be regenerated in order to have faith? These and related matters concerning the order of salvation have huge consequences for our understanding of the things of God and are by no means merely theological nit-picking.

When we examine the "golden chain" of Romans 8, we see that Paul mentioned not only foreknowledge and predestination but also calling, justification, and glorification. He said, "Moreover whom He predestined, these He also called; whom He called, these He also justified; and whom He justified, these He also glorified" (v. 30).

The literary order of Romans 8 is foreknowledge, predestination, calling, justification, and then glorification. The Apostle expressed the links in the chain by saying that those whom He predestined He also called, and those whom He called He also justified, and so on. The presumption of virtually every commentator on this text is that the word *whom* always refers to all of those in the class mentioned. That is, all whom God predestined are called, and all whom God calls are justified, and all whom God justifies are glorified. If this is the case, the text absolutely demolishes the prescient view of election.

Why would this text be so damaging to the prescient view? The answer lies in the relationship between calling and justification. What is the meaning of divine calling in this text? In theology, we distinguish between the *outward* call of God and the *inward* call of God. The outward call refers to the preaching of the gospel. When we preach, we give the outward call that some people respond to positively and others reject. Obviously not every person who hears the outward call responds to God in faith.

What about the inward call? This refers to the call of God the Holy Spirit to our souls. The abiding issue is whether this inward call is effectual. The theological school known as semi-Pelagianism teaches that the inward call is not necessarily effectual but can be resisted and rejected by the person who receives it. The person must cooperate with the inward call for faith to arise. In this schema, the inward call of God makes faith and justification possible but by no means certain. What is crucial for this theory is that not every person who receives the inward call comes to faith and is justified. Only some who are called in this sense are justified.

Conversely, in historic Augustinian theology, the grace of God's inward call is effectual. That is, it accomplishes its desired effect, and the sinner is brought to faith every time. All who receive the effectual inward call of God are justified. Since those who are called are also those who are justified, the plain sense of the text requires that the inward calling is an effectual calling.

If the text meant to teach the prescient view of election, it would have to say that *some* whom God foreknew He predestines, and *some* whom He calls He justifies, and *some* whom He justifies He glorifies. If the presumption of "all" is changed to "some," the result is not only confusing, but our entire understanding of salvation is thrown to the wind.

But if the Augustinian view of election is in view here, the text is consistent. All whom God foreknows in a certain way are predestined. All whom God predestines are called. All the called are justified. All the justified are glorified. The order of salvation begins with God's foreknowledge and extends all the way to the saints' glorification. The plan is God's plan, conceived and executed by Him from beginning to end, leaving us with the certain conclusion that salvation is of the Lord.

If all who are foreknown are predestined unto salvation, then the nature of this foreknowledge must be explained. If the "all" includes each and every human being, then clearly the text teaches a doctrine of universalism. If God sovereignly decrees and predestines all to salvation, if God is God, each and every person is saved.

On the other hand, if the "all" refers not to each and every person but to each and every person who is predestined unto salvation, the "all" has to do with a particular class. That is, "all" refers to all of the elect. This means that all who are foreknown by God as His elect are called, justified, and glorified.

That God foreknows His elect means far more than that He is intellectually aware of their existence before He creates them or that He knows their future actions. The "knowledge" of foreknowledge involves more than cognitive awareness.

When we study the nuances of the verb *to know* in New Testament Greek, we see striking and important differences in levels of knowing. For example, when Paul spoke of the condition of humanity with respect to its knowledge of God received through creation, he declared that humankind does know God:

> For the wrath of God is revealed from heaven against all ungodliness and unrighteousness of men, who suppress the truth in unrighteousness, because what may be known of God is manifest in them, for God has shown it to them. For since the creation of the world His invisible attributes are clearly seen, being understood by the things that are made, even His eternal power and Godhead, so that they are without excuse, because, although they knew God, they did not glorify Him as God, nor were thankful, but became futile in their thoughts, and their foolish hearts were darkened. (Rom. 1:18–21)

In this text, Paul spoke of "what may be known of God" (which is clear and manifest). He said that God's attributes are "understood." Finally and most conclusively, he said that "although they knew God, they did not glorify Him as God." In Romans 1, Paul saw the universal sin of humanity not in our refusal to know God but in our refusal to glorify Him as God. Paul made it clear that God's revelation of Himself in nature gets through and yields some knowledge of the Creator, enough knowledge to leave the creature without excuse. The excuse of ignorance is demolished. No one can plead before God that he or she was ignorant of God's existence. Since this knowledge gets through, we must conclude that at the very least fallen humanity has a cognitive knowledge of God. In this regard, is it then accurate to declare that all people possess some knowledge or some kind of knowledge of God?

However strongly Paul asserted that people have a knowledge of God from the revelation of Himself in and through nature, he elsewhere declared that natural humanity does not know God:

> Even so no one knows the things of God except the Spirit of God. Now we have received, not the spirit of the world, but the Spirit who is from God, that we might know the things that have been freely given to us by God.
>
> These things we also speak, not in words which man's wisdom teaches but which the Holy Spirit teaches, comparing spiritual things with spiritual. But the natural man does not receive the things of the Spirit of God, for they are foolishness to him; nor can he know them, because they are spiritually discerned. (1 Cor. 2:11–14)

Here Paul spoke of a certain inability of natural humanity to know the things of God. In one sense, no one knows God or can know God unless the Holy Spirit makes God known to that person. Was Paul then speaking in contradictions? Was he teaching one thing in Romans and its direct opposite in 1 Corinthians? By no means. The knowledge of which he spoke in 1 Corinthians is a knowledge that goes beyond and is different from the mere cognitive apprehension alluded to in Romans. This knowledge is a salvific knowledge, an intimate personal knowledge that is conveyed by the Holy Spirit and experienced only by the believer.

In the Old Testament, this deeper level of "knowing" is expressed in the use of the verb *to know* as a term for sexual intercourse. For example, in Genesis 4 we read, "Now Adam knew Eve his wife, and she conceived and bore … Cain." Scripture is not merely engaging in euphemism. Neither is it teaching that Eve became pregnant the moment Adam had a cognitive awareness of her existence. That Adam "knew" his wife here means that he knew her in the most intimate way possible for human beings to know each other (at least in terms of physical intimacy).

Therefore, understanding that the verb *to know* is used biblically at more than one level, how are we to understand the kind of knowledge that is in the foreknowledge of the golden chain? I suggest that here God's foreknowledge of those whom He predestines to salvation is not merely a prior cognitive awareness of their names but a prior redemptive love for them, the salvific love that He bestowed on Jacob but not on Esau. Because the distinction in God's actions toward Jacob and Esau is a distinction between love and hate, and because Paul stated clearly that this distinction was present before they were born, we must say that God foreloved Jacob.

Since Romans 9 expresses concretely that which Paul expressed somewhat abstractly in the golden chain, I think it is safe to conclude that the foreknowing of the chain is a foreloving. This means then that the grace of God in election is a manifestation of the love of God. The electing God is a loving God, and the loving God is an electing God.

When we discuss the difficult doctrine of predestination, we must keep in mind that our election is always an election in Christ and to Christ. Remember that a qualifying statement appears right in the midst of the golden chain: "For whom He foreknew, He also predestined to be conformed to the image of His Son, that He might be the firstborn among many brethren" (Rom. 8:29). Predestination is said to be for the purpose of being conformed to the image of Christ. This is what is accomplished ultimately in our glorification. Glorification is the consummation of our sanctification, the final purification from all sin.

However, our conformity to the image of Christ is the penultimate purpose here. The ultimate purpose, indicated by the last of the purpose clauses of the text, is that Christ might be the firstborn of many brethren. This brings us squarely back to the doctrine of adoption. This brings us back to the Father's profound love for His Son, which causes us to be adopted not only in Christ but also *for* Christ. So, then, we are not only elected in Christ and to Christ but ultimately for Christ. We are the gifts the Father gives to the Son. We are the gifts of the Father's love for His Son.

THE FATHER'S GIFT TO THE SON

Jesus expressed the motif of the elect as a gift to the Son on various occasions, particularly in the gospel of John: "This is the will of the

Father who sent Me, that of all He has given Me I should lose nothing, but should raise it up at the last day. And this is the will of Him who sent Me, that everyone who sees the Son and believes in Him may have everlasting life; and I will raise him up at the last day" (6:39–40). In this passage, Jesus made it clear that He is concerned about every believer being raised up at the last day. This qualifies His statement that what the Father has given Him will never be lost. Believers are given to Christ by the Father, and these believers will never be lost.

This affirmation builds on what Jesus declared only moments earlier: "But I said to you that you have seen Me and yet do not believe. All that the Father gives Me will come to Me, and the one who comes to Me I will by no means cast out. For I have come down from heaven, not to do My own will, but the will of Him who sent Me" (6:36–38). Jesus was emphatic in His assertion that all whom the Father gives to Him will in fact come to Him. The order here is crucial. Jesus did not say that all who come to Him will then be given to Him by the Father. We do not determine by our response who will be the Father's gift to the Son. Rather, our response is determined by the prior election of God for us to come to the Son as gifts to Him.

The concept of believers being the gifts of the Father to the Son forms a central element of Jesus's high priestly prayer in John 17. Jesus here made reference to this "giving": "Father, the hour has come. Glorify Your Son, that Your Son also may glorify You, as You have given Him authority over all flesh, that He should give eternal life to as many as You have given Him" (vv. 1–2).

Christ went on to speak of the authority He received from the Father to grant eternal life to certain people. Those people are the ones the Father has given to Him:

I have manifested Your name to the men whom You have given Me out of the world. They were Yours, You gave them to Me, and they have kept Your word. Now they have known that all things which You have given Me are from You. For I have given to them the words which You have given Me; and they have received them, and have known surely that I came forth from You; and they have believed that You sent Me.

I pray for them. I do not pray for the world but for those whom You have given Me, for they are Yours. And all Mine are Yours, and Yours are Mine, and I am glorified in them. Now I am no longer in the world, but these are in the world, and I come to You. Holy Father, keep through Your name those whom You have given Me, that they may be one as We are. While I was with them in the world, I kept them in Your name. Those whom You gave Me I have kept; and none of them is lost except the son of perdition, that the Scripture might be fulfilled. (vv. 6–12)

In this prayer, it is clear that believers are the Father's gift to the Son, a gift that is not to be lost or destroyed. Jesus prayed that these gifts may be kept and not discarded. He thanked the Father that all have been kept except the son of perdition, who is elsewhere described as having been a devil (John 6:70). The son of perdition is Judas (John 6:71).

The concept of our adoption in Christ as the Father's gift to the Son is also declared by the author of Hebrews:

For it was fitting for Him, for whom are all things and by whom are all things, in bringing many sons to glory, to make the captain of their salvation perfect through sufferings. For both He who sanctifies and those who are being sanctified are all of one, for which reason He is not ashamed to call them brethren, saying:

"I will declare Your name to My brethren;
In the midst of the assembly I will sing praise to You."

And again:

"I will put My trust in Him."

And again:

"Here am I and the children whom God has given Me."
(2:10–13)

This text confirms that the elect are given to Christ as His adopted brothers and the Father's adopted children. This is the astonishing love that would provoke John to utter later, "Behold what manner of love the Father has bestowed on us, that we should be called children of God!" (1 John 3:1).

CHAPTER 7

THE THREEFOLD LOVE OF GOD

Historically, three different types of the love of God have been distinguished. The first is His love of benevolence. The second is His love of beneficence. The third is His love of complacency. All three of these are grounded in and flow out of the goodness of God.

THE LOVE OF BENEVOLENCE

The word *benevolence* is derived from the combination of the Latin prefix *bene*, which means "well" or "good," and the Latin root that means "will." Together the prefix and the root mean "goodwill." We see that the benevolent love of God refers to His goodwill toward His creatures.

In the narrative of Jesus's birth in Luke's gospel we read:

> Now there were in the same country shepherds living out in the fields, keeping watch over their flock by night. And behold, an angel of the Lord stood before them, and the glory of the Lord shone around them, and they were greatly afraid. Then the angel said to them, "Do not be afraid, for behold, I bring you good tidings of great joy which will be to all people. For there is born to you this day in the city of David a Savior, who is Christ the Lord. And this will be the sign to you: You will find a Babe wrapped in swaddling cloths, lying in a manger."
>
> And suddenly there was with the angel a multitude of the heavenly host praising God and saying:

> "Glory to God in the highest,
> And on earth peace, goodwill toward men!" (2:8–14)

The spectacular sound and light show that took place in the fields outside Bethlehem on the night of Christ's birth included the angelic announcement of peace on earth and goodwill toward men. The incarnation was an expression of the goodwill of God, His benevolent love. Christ came into the world not only by the will of the Father but also by the goodwill of the Father. Of course, the only kind of will God has is a good will. There is no evil in Him or any malevolence in His will.

The link between the benevolence of God and His love is seen in John 3:16–17: "For God so loved the world that He gave His only begotten Son, that whoever believes in Him should not perish but have everlasting life. For God did not send His Son into the world to condemn the world, but that the world through Him might be saved." God's sending of Christ into the world was an expression of His love and of the goodness of His will.

In the political realm, we sometimes hear of a "benevolent dictator." Such a phrase may sound like an oxymoron, but it is not. It is possible for a ruler who has absolute power to rule his domain with goodness and justice. He may be a person of goodwill with a genuine concern for the well-being of his subjects. Though rare, such rulers are not altogether unheard of. It may be said of God that He is the quintessential benevolent dictator. He possesses absolute power, but His power is directed not for the purpose of crushing His subjects but for expressing His goodness and goodwill toward them.

When the New Testament speaks of the will of God, the word *will* is highly nuanced. Scripture speaks of the will of God in different ways. In the first instance, the Bible speaks of it in the sense of His sovereign decretive will by which He brings to pass whatsoever He commands. When God commanded the light to shine in His work of creation, by His very call the light began to shine. When He said, "Let there be light," there was light (Gen. 1:3). The light could not resist the sovereign will of God. The light had to shine in the face of this decree.

But the Bible also speaks of the will of God in the preceptive sense. The preceptive will of God refers to His Law or His moral commands, His divine precepts. The preceptive will of God differs from His decretive will. Though creatures are powerless to disobey or thwart the decretive will, they are able to disobey the preceptive will. Sometimes this aspect of the divine will is called God's *permissive* will in that He "allows" or "lets" the sinner sin. The term *permissive* is a bit dangerous, as it seems to suggest that God gives His blessing to or somehow sanctions sin. On the contrary, when God "permits" our sins, it means that He lets us exercise our bad wills with bad actions. To be sure, He could stop us, but He chooses not to.

The preceptive will expresses what God commands us to do. It does not, however, compel our obedience. In this sense, we say that the preceptive will differs from His decretive will.

There is another way in which the Bible speaks of the will of God, which is the dispositional will of God. This refers to His divine attitude toward His creatures. God is not ill disposed toward people; rather, He is fundamentally well disposed toward us. In this sense, His good disposition is a manifestation of His benevolent love.

BENEVOLENCE AND ELECTION

Many who struggle with the doctrine of election point to the benevolent love of God as proof of the falsehood of the Augustinian view of election. Arminians argue that God is so constrained by His benevolent love that He saves as many people as He possibly can. This is not an argument for universalism because Arminians suppose that God cannot save some people no matter how well disposed He is toward them. Since they do not choose to be saved, God cannot overrule their choices, because to do so would be to violate their wills. Since some people remain willfully ill disposed toward God, they are not saved, even though God is well disposed toward them, according to this view.

The most common biblical text used to support this view is in 2 Peter: "But, beloved, do not forget this one thing, that with the Lord one day is as a thousand years, and a thousand years as one day. The Lord is not slack concerning His promise, as some count slackness, but is longsuffering toward us, not willing that any should perish but that all should come to repentance" (3:8–9).

For this text to demolish the Augustinian view of election, two assumptions must be established. The first is that the "willing" here refers to the decretive will of God and that "any" refers to any person. However, if that is the case, the text would demolish not only the Augustinian view of election but the Arminian view as well. If the "willing" here refers to the sovereign will of God and the "any" refers to all people, it would prove too much for the Arminian. Why? If this text means that God is not sovereignly or decretively willing that any person should perish, then manifestly no person would or could ever perish. The text would prove universalism, which neither Augustinian nor Arminian theology embraces.

One way to avoid the difficulty is to understand the "willing" of this text as referring not to the decretive will of God but to His will of disposition. That is, the divine benevolence is so great that God is utterly indisposed toward anyone's perishing. For someone to actually perish is an affront to God's love of benevolence.

This manner of interpreting the text has some support elsewhere in the Bible: "Therefore you, O son of man, say to the house of Israel:

'Thus you say, "If our transgressions and our sins lie upon us, and we pine away in them, how can we then live?"' Say to them: 'As I live,' says the Lord GOD, 'I have no pleasure in the death of the wicked, but that the wicked turn from his way and live. Turn, turn from your evil ways! For why should you die, O house of Israel?'" (Ezek. 33:10–11).

God made it clear that He takes no pleasure or delight in the death of the wicked. He remains benevolent in His attitude toward them. This would be a parallel idea to the notion that God's dispositional will is "for" rather than "against" the wicked. However, it is urgent for us to remember that even though God takes no pleasure in the death of the wicked, He still condemns the wicked to death. In the preceding passage of Ezekiel we read:

> So you, son of man: I have made you a watchman for
> the house of Israel; therefore you shall hear a word
> from My mouth and warn them for Me. When I say
> to the wicked, "O wicked man, you shall surely die!"
> and you do not speak to warn the wicked from his way,
> that wicked man shall die in his iniquity; but his blood
> I will require at your hand. Nevertheless if you warn
> the wicked to turn from his way, and he does not turn
> from his way, he shall die in his iniquity; but you have
> delivered your soul. (33:7–9)

By way of analogy, consider a judge who takes no personal delight in sentencing prisoners to death but who nevertheless issues such sentences to uphold the law and to establish justice. God takes no pleasure in sending the wicked to their just punishment, but He does will their punishment, else they would never receive it.

THE IMPASSIBILITY OF GOD

When we speak of God's will of disposition, we are quickly confronted with questions raised by the classic doctrine of the impassibility of God. Sometimes the impassibility of God is expressed philosophically in such a way as to describe God as a being utterly incapable of feeling. In a desire to protect the immutability of God, to free Him from all passions that would be dependent on the actions of the creature, and to ensure the constant and abiding state of pure and total felicity in God, He is regarded as having no feelings. This robs God of His personal character and reduces Him to an impersonal force or blob of cosmic energy.

This kind of impassibility makes a mockery of the biblical revelation of the character of God. It is one thing to ensure that God is not subject to mood swings by which His beatific state is disturbed or destroyed, or to passions that cause perturbations in His character. However, we must not let a speculative form of impassibility strip God of His personal attributes, especially His attribute of love. We do not need to embrace either the patripassian heresy (whereby the Father suffers in the death of Christ) or the theopaschitist heresy (whereby the divine nature of Christ suffers and dies on the cross) in order to affirm the reality of affection in God. If there is no feeling in God, there can be no affection in Him. If He has no capacity for affection, He has no capacity for love.

But the Bible is filled with references to the feelings of God. Though they may represent anthropomorphic ideas and employ the language of analogy, they are certainly not meaningless. Consider the words of the psalmist:

> The LORD is merciful and gracious,
> Slow to anger, and abounding in mercy.
> He will not always strive with us,
> Nor will He keep His anger forever.
> He has not dealt with us according to our sins,
> Nor punished us according to our iniquities.
>
> For as the heavens are high above the earth,
> So great is His mercy toward those who fear Him;
> As far as the east is from the west,
> So far has He removed our transgressions from us.
> As a father pities his children,
> So the LORD pities those who fear Him. (103:8–13)

An analogy is used here to describe God's pity for His people. It is likened to the pity a human father feels for his children. This does not mean there is a direct correspondence between God's pity and people's pity. They are not identical, but they are similar in some way and to some degree. If there is no analogy, then the biblical statement is both meaningless and worthless. The message that comes through the Scriptures loud and clear is that in some way analogous to human concern and feeling, God cares for us. This truth must never be abandoned to satisfy philosophical speculation.

If, then, we can speak of a true disposition that may be found in God, and this disposition is a benevolent one, how do we understand the teaching of Peter that God is not willing that any should perish? I think the answer lies chiefly in the meaning of the word *any*. To interpret this nonspecific *any* to refer to any human being involves making an inference from the text that is not called for. Peter does not explicitly declare what or which "any" he means. If we examine the text closely, it is clear that the term *any* is hanging in the text without definition. The immediate antecedent of *any* is the word "us."

Let us look at the passage again: "But, beloved, do not forget this one thing, that with the Lord one day is as a thousand years, and a thousand years as one day. The Lord is not slack concerning His promise, as some count slackness, but is longsuffering toward us, not willing that any should perish but that all should come to repentance" (2 Pet. 3:8–9). We note that Peter declared that God is long suffering toward "us," not willing that any of *us* should perish. The "us" includes those whom Peter addressed at the beginning of verse 8 as "beloved." Who are these beloved to whom Peter spoke?

At the very beginning of chapter 3, he also addressed his readers as "beloved" and reminded them that this letter was his second epistle sent in order to stir up their minds. If we then go back to the first epistle of Peter, we see that it opens with these words: "To the pilgrims of the Dispersion in Pontus, Galatia, Cappadocia, Asia, and Bithynia, elect according to the foreknowledge of God the Father, in sanctification of the Spirit, for obedience and sprinkling of the blood of Jesus Christ" (1:1–2). Peter addressed his first epistle, and by extension his second as well, to the elect. That is why, in the second epistle, he exhorted his readers to be diligent to "make your call and election sure" (1:10).

The doctrine of election was not foreign to the Apostle Peter. His assertion that God is not willing that any should perish does not negate the Augustinian view of election but confirms it. The willing in view may be seen as God's sovereign, efficacious will that solidifies our hope in our full redemption without teaching universalism. This text shows the benevolence of God, His goodwill to His beloved elect in Christ.

THE LOVE OF BENEFICENCE

The primary difference between benevolence and beneficence is the difference between willing and doing. Just as God's love includes His goodwill, it also includes His good actions in behalf of the creature. Out of His goodwill flow good deeds. He differs sharply from us in that all of His deeds are perfect in their goodness, just as all of His will is perfect. God never endures the kind of struggle within Himself that Paul recorded in Romans 7:

> For we know that the law is spiritual, but I am carnal, sold under sin. For what I am doing, I do not understand. For what I will to do, that I do not practice; but what I hate, that I do. If, then, I do what I will not to do, I agree with the law that it is good. But now, it is no longer I who do it, but sin that dwells in me. For I know that in me (that is, in my flesh) nothing

good dwells; for to will is present with me, but how to perform what is good I do not find. For the good that I will to do, I do not do; but the evil I will not to do, that I practice. Now if I do what I will not to do, it is no longer I who do it, but sin that dwells in me.

I find then a law, that evil is present with me, the one who wills to do good. For I delight in the law of God according to the inward man. But I see another law in my members, warring against the law of my mind, and bringing me into captivity to the law of sin which is in my members. (vv. 14–23)

The warfare Paul depicted was a struggle between his own goodwill and bad will. When his bad will prevailed, he did what was evil. In a word, he sinned. He said that the good that he willed to do he did not do. This disjunction between willing and doing is unique to fallen humanity; it has no place in the character of God.

The link between willing and doing is shown in the way God's love works itself out. Because of His goodwill toward us, we receive the benefits of His loving-kindness. This is a vital element of His providential government of the world. In the Sermon on the Mount, Jesus spoke of this beneficent providence:

You have heard that it was said, "You shall love your neighbor and hate your enemy." But I say to you, love your enemies, bless those who curse you, do good to those who hate you, and pray for those who spitefully use you and persecute you, that you may be sons of your Father in heaven; for He makes His sun rise on the evil and on the good, and sends rain on the just and on the unjust. For if you love those who love you, what reward have you? Do not even the tax collectors do the same? And if you greet your brethren only, what do you do more than others? Do not even the tax collectors do so? Therefore you shall be perfect, just as your Father in heaven is perfect. (Matt. 5:43–48)

It is important to observe that the context of Jesus's teaching on the providential care of God is His exhortation to love not only our neighbor but our enemy as well. When He said we should do this, He indicated that the purpose is that we may be the sons of our heavenly Father. To be an adopted son of God is to be an obedient son of God.

Often in Scripture, sonship is defined not so much in terms of biological lineage as in terms of obedience. This was the issue in Jesus's dispute with the Pharisees:

As He spoke these words, many believed in Him.

Then Jesus said to those Jews who believed Him, "If you abide in My word, you are My disciples indeed. And you shall know the truth, and the truth shall make you free."

They answered Him, "We are Abraham's descendants, and have never been in bondage to anyone. How can you say, 'You will be made free'?"

Jesus answered them, "Most assuredly, I say to you,

whoever commits sin is a slave of sin. And a slave does not abide in the house forever, but a son abides forever. Therefore if the Son makes you free, you shall be free indeed.

"I know that you are Abraham's descendants, but you seek to kill Me, because My word has no place in you. I speak what I have seen with My Father, and you do what you have seen with your father."

They answered and said to Him, "Abraham is our father."

Jesus said to them, "If you were Abraham's children, you would do the works of Abraham. But now you seek to kill Me, a Man who has told you the truth which I heard from God. Abraham did not do this. You do the deeds of your father."

Then they said to Him, "We were not born of fornication; we have one Father—God."

Jesus said to them, "If God were your Father, you would love Me, for I proceeded forth and came from God; nor have I come of Myself, but He sent Me. Why do you not understand My speech? Because you are not able to listen to My word. You are of your father the devil, and the desires of your father you want to do." (John 8:30–44)

The Pharisees were insulted when Jesus spoke of being made free by the Son. They claimed to have Abraham for their father and, being the descendants of Abraham, they were in bondage to no man. Jesus replied: "If you were Abraham's children, you would do the works of Abraham." In this statement Jesus argued from the link between sonship and obedience. Anyone who was a true son of Abraham would behave as Abraham did.

As the debate heated up, the Pharisees switched their claim from being the children of Abraham to being the children of God. They cried out, "We were not born of fornication; we have one Father— God." Jesus challenged this claim by saying, "If God were your Father, you would love Me, for I proceeded forth and came from God; nor have I come of Myself, but He sent Me."

The idea here is that sonship involves obeying the Father by loving what the Father loves. Since the Father loved His beloved Son, it was inconceivable to Jesus that anyone could be a child of the Father and at the same time hate the Father's beloved Son. Jesus declared that the Pharisees were so far from being children of God that they were actually children of the Devil. He said, "You are of your father the devil, and the desires of your father you want to do."

At the end of this discourse with the Pharisees, Jesus concluded by saying, "But because I tell the truth, you do not believe Me. Which of you convicts Me of sin? And if I tell the truth, why do you not believe Me? He who is of God hears God's words; therefore you do not hear, because you are not of God" (John 8:45–47).

The one who is of God hears God. He loves what God loves and does what God requires him to do. This is the essence of sonship.

It is this sonship of which Jesus spoke in the Sermon on the Mount. To love your neighbor *and* your enemy is to be a child of the heavenly Father, because this is precisely what God Himself does. His benefits accrue not only to believers but also to unbelievers.

When people remain at enmity with God, they do so while they are receiving benefits from His hand.

When Jesus commanded us to love our enemies, He defined that love not so much in terms of feelings of affection as in terms of actions. To love our enemies requires that we bless them when they curse us and do good to them when they hate us. This is what it means to reflect the love of God, because God does good to those who hate Him and blesses people while they curse Him.

Jesus illustrated the beneficent love of God by pointing to the sun and the rain. God makes His sun rise on the wicked as well as the good, and He sends rain on both the just and the unjust. When we experience a rain shower, we do not see the raindrops falling with personal discrimination. We do not see bad people getting wet and good people walking through the shower untouched. The righteous and the wicked both need an umbrella. At the same time, the wicked farmer and the righteous farmer receive refreshment for their fields. Sun and storm alike affect both.

The bestowal of the benefits of God on both the wicked and the righteous is called in theology "common grace." Common grace is called "grace" because all of the benefits that flow from the holy God are undeserved. All the good things we receive from the hand of God are gifts. They are not rewards earned by our merit. Grace, by definition, means the undeserved or unmerited favor of God. These favors are poured out from His bounty on believer and unbeliever alike. The air that we breathe, the food that we eat, and the water that we drink are all benefits that come from Him. Perhaps it is in recognition that He owes us none of these things that we call the prayer of thanksgiving that accompanies a meal "saying grace." Of course, the common grace of God includes far more than the daily necessities of life. At times, the gifts of His common grace are poured out in abundance and may include great prosperity for its recipients. All that we have are gifts from this treasure house of common grace.

Common grace is called "common" because it is distinguished from "special" grace, which is the grace of salvation. Special grace is what God extends to His elect, by which they are brought into His family through adoption. On the other hand, all people, commonly, receive the benefits of common grace.

There is irony here, however. The gifts of God's common grace, which flow out of His benevolence and beneficence, which are blessings for the moment, actually become occasions for judgment for the wicked. Every time an impenitent person receives a gift from God with ingratitude, he or she heaps up wrath against the day of judgment (Rom. 2:5). But God does not give these gifts to torment the sinner. They are truly beneficial. They become nonbeneficial in the long run only because of the obstinate sinfulness of the wicked. But the misuse and abuse of the good gifts of God do not make them bad gifts.

The beneficent love of God is seen in the way God in His providence graciously provides for the needs of nature and people. Jesus reiterated this near the end of the Sermon on the Mount:

> Therefore I say to you, do not worry about your life, what you will eat or what you will drink; nor about your body, what you will put on. Is not life more than food and the body more than clothing? Look at the birds of the air, for they neither sow nor reap nor gather into barns; yet your heavenly Father feeds them.

Are you not of more value than they? Which of you by worrying can add one cubit to his stature?

So why do you worry about clothing? Consider the lilies of the field, how they grow: they neither toil nor spin; and yet I say to you that even Solomon in all his glory was not arrayed like one of these. Now if God so clothes the grass of the field, which today is, and tomorrow is thrown into the oven, will He not much more clothe you, O you of little faith?

Therefore do not worry, saying, "What shall we eat?" or "What shall we drink?" or "What shall we wear?" For after all these things the Gentiles seek. For your heavenly Father knows that you need all these things. But seek first the kingdom of God and His righteousness, and all these things shall be added to you. Therefore do not worry about tomorrow, for tomorrow will worry about its own things. Sufficient for the day is its own trouble. (Matt. 6:25–34)

The gifts of divine providence are truly good gifts and not the ploys of an ill-tempered deity who takes delight in giving gifts to sinners merely so He can increase their punishment.

THE LOVE OF COMPLACENCY

The third type of the love of God is His love of complacency. This type of love is a bit more difficult to define than His love of benevolence or beneficence. The chief reason is because of the common meaning of the word *complacency*. We tend to think of complacency as a lack of concern about things. It is likened to being "at ease in Zion," being comfortable in a smug way, resting on past laurels and having no cares for any impending danger.

This notion of complacency has little to do with the theological concept of God's love of complacency. In theological language, the term *complacent* is used more in line with its etymology than with its current usage. The Latin root originally meant "to please greatly." In this sense, God's love of complacency means that He is greatly pleased with His children.

When we examined the Father's love for the Son, we looked at the audible announcement the Father made from heaven at Jesus's baptism: "When all the people were baptized, it came to pass that Jesus also was baptized; and while He prayed, the heaven was opened. And the Holy Spirit descended in bodily form like a dove upon Him, and a voice came from heaven which said, 'You are My beloved Son; in You I am well pleased'" (Luke 3:21–22). When the Father declared from heaven that He was "well pleased" with His Son, He was declaring His love of complacency for Him.

Classical theologians saw this love of complacency as the delight God has for His creatures who manifest His image. Of course, nowhere is this image of God so clearly and marvelously shown as in the person of Christ. The author of Hebrews said:

> God, who at various times and in various ways spoke
> in time past to the fathers by the prophets, has in
> these last days spoken to us by His Son, whom He

has appointed heir of all things, through whom also He made the worlds; who being the brightness of His glory and the express image of His person, and upholding all things by the word of His power, when He had by Himself purged our sins, sat down at the right hand of the Majesty on high, having become so much better than the angels, as He has by inheritance obtained a more excellent name than they. (1:1–4)

The three types of divine love may also be understood in terms of three degrees of God's love. The love of benevolence refers to His goodwill toward the creature from eternity past. His love of beneficence is expressed in time and space, and His love of complacency reflects His love in the creature's redeemed state. Another way of saying this is that, by His love of benevolence, God loved us before we existed; by His love of beneficence, He loves us as we are; and by His love of complacency, He loves us when we are renewed after the image of Christ.

By God's goodwill, we are elected. By His beneficence, we are redeemed. By His complacency, we are rewarded in heaven. It is by His love of complacency that He will say to us, "Well done, good and faithful servant" (Matt. 25:21).

The manifestation of the future love of God was hinted at by the prophet Isaiah:

> For Zion's sake I will not hold My peace,
> And for Jerusalem's sake I will not rest,
> Until her righteousness goes forth as brightness,

And her salvation as a lamp that burns.
The Gentiles shall see your righteousness,
And all kings your glory.
You shall be called by a new name,
Which the mouth of the LORD will name.
You shall also be a crown of glory
In the hand of the LORD,
And a royal diadem
In the hand of your God. (62:1–3)

According to this promise, the people of God not only will receive a crown of glory from Him, but also will *be* a crown of glory to Him. They will receive a new name from His divine mouth.

Such rewards will flow out of God's love of complacency. He will express His loving pleasure toward His saints. Again, this takes place within the broader context of God's adopting love. The rewards that He gives are not according to their merits but according to the merits of Christ. Whatever deeds we do as Christians we do as a result of His grace working in us. Because of the gracious character of these works, we have nothing of which to boast in ourselves.

Often the biblical doctrine of justification by faith alone is misunderstood to mean that good works have nothing to do with the Christian life. On the contrary, they have everything to do with the Christian life, as they are essential to our sanctification. The doctrine of justification by faith alone teaches that our works contribute nothing to our justification. Our justification rests squarely on the works of Christ alone. But we can still say that though we are justified by faith alone, our rewards in heaven are distributed according to our works. This "according to" does not mean that our works merit a reward. They do not. Our best works remain tainted with sin to such a degree that Augustine called them "splendid vices." Augustine also taught that when God rewards our works in heaven, this is a reward of grace and is, as it were, God's crowning His own work.

Since our election is unto conformity to Christ and unto good works, we see the love of God working in our redemption from beginning to end, from election to the divine initiative by which we are brought to Christ, to the end goal of our glorification, in which God expresses His love of complacency.

This progress of faith is mentioned in Hebrews:

> By faith Abel offered to God a more excellent sacrifice than Cain, through which he obtained witness that he was righteous, God testifying of his gifts; and through it he being dead still speaks.
>
> By faith Enoch was taken away so that he did not see death, "and was not found, because God had taken him"; for before he was taken he had this testimony, that he pleased God. But without faith it is impossible to please Him, for he who comes to God must believe that He is, and that He is a rewarder of those who diligently seek Him.
>
> By faith Noah, being divinely warned of things not yet seen, moved with godly fear, prepared an ark for the saving of his household, by which he condemned the world and became heir of the righteousness which is according to faith. (11:4–7)

That Enoch pleased God by his faith indicates his reception of God's love of complacency. Yet what occurred with Enoch is not an isolated case. The same love of complacency is directed to all who are believers—but only to believers. The text makes it clear that without faith it is impossible to please God. And without the divine pleasure, there can be no divine love of complacency, because divine pleasure *is* the love of complacency.

The author of Hebrews declared that God is a rewarder of those who diligently seek Him. Yet, it is only the believer who diligently seeks God. Paul taught that by nature no one seeks after God (Rom. 3:11). The seeking of God begins at conversion; it does not end there. It is the regenerate person who seeks God and makes seeking after God the main business of his or her life. And that lifelong quest is accompanied by the complacent love of God.

CHAPTER 8

AGAPE LOVE

Many Christians have heard sermons in which the preacher explained the meanings of three different Greek words for "love." These words have sometimes been confused, as either too much or too little was made of their distinctions. What follows is a summary of the definitions of these words as supplied by Ethelbert Stauffer in his technical essay in the first volume of Gerhard Kittel and Gerhard Friedrich's *Theological Dictionary of the New Testament.*

In this essay, Stauffer canvassed the three Greek terms—*eros, philein,* and *agape*—as they functioned in prebiblical Greek. The term *eros,* which was also the name of a Greek deity, describes a passionate love of a joyous sensuality or even of a demonic orientation. The cultic worship of Eros involved orgiastic frenzies of intoxication and sexual indulgence. The goal was a kind of religious or mystical experience of transcendence. The frenzy liberated the worshipper from the constraints of rationality or even volition. He became gripped in the power of Eros, experiencing a supreme bliss and ecstasy. These celebrations were also linked to cultic fertility rites and the practice of temple prostitution.

In later periods, *eros* was cleansed of its purely sensual orientation and became a symbol for a mystical encounter with the spiritual realm. Both Plato and Aristotle sought to free *eros* from the sensual and the demonic, and fill it with a spiritual love of the soul.

The second word for "love" was *philein*. This term was generally used for the love between friends. This is the word that undergirds the name of the city Philadelphia. The "City of Brotherly Love" is so called because its name derives from the Greek word *philein* joined with the Greek word for "brother," *adelphos*.

The third word for "love" was *agape*. This word underwent a significant development between its prebiblical usage and its usage in the New Testament and the early church. To the Greek, there was no supernatural or mystical power in *agape*. It referred simply to an inward attitude of satisfaction with something. Sometimes it indicated a sense of personal esteem or preference. It was applied to the feelings of one person for another, such as a parent's affection for an only child.

As the word was processed through Judaism, it took on a much deeper significance. It was used to translate the Old Testament concept of love, including the love of God. But the term was further enriched by Jesus's use of it in the New Testament.

JESUS'S USE OF *AGAPE*

Jesus summed up the Old Testament law in terms of the demand to love God and to love one's neighbor. The love that is commanded for God is unconditional. Here we find an authentic kind of unconditional love in the Bible. There is no condition God must meet before we are under obligation to love Him with all our heart, soul, strength, and mind. He is altogether worthy of that love. All creatures, who owe their very existence to their Creator, who live and move and have their being in that Creator, owe honor and esteem to Him.

The call to love God is decisive. It involves a radical mandate to be in subjection to His lordship. This is seen in Jesus's teaching regarding the unprofitable servant:

> And which of you, having a servant plowing or tending sheep, will say to him when he has come in from the field, "Come at once and sit down to eat"? But will he not rather say to him, "Prepare something for my supper, and gird yourself and serve me till I have eaten and drunk, and afterward you will eat and drink"? Does he thank that servant because he did the things that were commanded him? I think not. So likewise you, when you have done all those things which you are commanded, say, "We are unprofitable servants. We have done what was our duty to do." (Luke 17:7–10)

This parable seems a bit harsh at first glance, but it reveals a profound lesson about our obligation to obey God. Will the master indicate his indebtedness to a servant who has simply done his duty? By no means. The point Jesus made is that there is nothing we can do that is above the call of duty. All obedience we render to God is simply a matter of obligation. To love God is to enact the role of the slave before his master.

The slave-master motif is found throughout the New Testament. The Apostle Paul characteristically identified himself as a slave of the Lord Jesus Christ. The slave is owned by his master. He cannot come and go as he pleases. Paul extended the analogy beyond himself to the whole Christian community when he declared that we are not our own but have been bought with a price. The price of our purchase was the blood of Christ, the value of which exceeds any amount of silver or gold.

One of the most neglected texts of the New Testament is found in Paul's letter to the Ephesians:

> Bondservants, be obedient to those who are your masters according to the flesh, with fear and trembling, in sincerity of heart, as to Christ; not with eyeservice, as men-pleasers, but as bondservants of Christ, doing the will of God from the heart, with goodwill doing service, as to the Lord, and not to men, knowing that whatever good anyone does, he will receive the same from the Lord, whether he is a slave or free.
>
> And you, masters, do the same things to them, giving up threatening, knowing that your own Master also is in heaven, and there is no partiality with Him. (6:5–9)

This text tends to be ignored because slavery has been abolished in the Western world. The text follows a series of injunctions that define certain relationships. The call to wives to be in subjection to their husbands has been studied with great rigor in light of the feminist movement. But this section regarding slaves and their masters is glossed over as being irrelevant to modern times. However, since we are called to be slaves to Christ in manifesting our love for Him, instructions to slaves in the physical world have some application to those who enter into slavery in the spiritual realm.

The obedience that is called for here is to be marked by "fear and trembling." Paul was speaking here of a godly fear, such as every Christian is called to manifest in working out his or her salvation, as the Apostle declared to the Philippians (2:12). It is also an obedience that is to be rendered "in sincerity of heart, as to Christ." The slave was to offer obedience to the master as if offering it to Christ Himself. In our spiritual slavery to Christ, there is no "as if." Our obedience is always offered directly to Him. This is our reply to His command "If you love Me, keep My commandments" (John 14:15). The obedience that flows from a sincerity of heart is an obedience that flows from love.

Next the Apostle contrasted sincere obedience with its negation. That is, he proceeded to show what sincere obedience is not. It is "not [done] with eyeservice, as men-pleasers." Servants who give the obedience of eyeservice work only when the master is looking over their shoulders. Such servants or workers always need a "supervisor" (one who looks over them) to perform their appointed tasks. If left without such supervision, these servants shirk their duties and slack off in their labors. Further, they are "men-pleasers," those who play to the crowd, living out life as political opportunists. They work for the applause of men and not for the approval of God.

The spiritual slave of Christ who offers obedience born of *agape* cannot function as a man-pleaser. To be a man-pleaser or a politician in the pejorative sense is to deny one's servant relationship to Christ. Paul made that clear when he took the Galatians to task over the truth of the gospel:

> I marvel that you are turning away so soon from Him who called you in the grace of Christ, to a different gospel, which is not another; but there are some who trouble you and want to pervert the gospel of Christ. But even if we, or an angel from heaven, preach any other gospel to you than what we have preached to you, let him be accursed. As we have said before, so now I say again, if anyone preaches any other gospel to you than what you have received, let him be accursed.
>
> For do I now persuade men, or God? Or do I seek to please men? For if I still pleased men, I would not be a bondservant of Christ. (Gal. 1:6–10)

In this controversy, Paul found it necessary to rebuke Peter to his face and to call Barnabas back to fidelity to the gospel (Gal. 2:11–13). Paul indicated here that he faced the dilemma of pleasing his coworkers or pleasing God. He came down on the side of pleasing God rather than people, knowing that being a servant of Christ allowed no other alternative.

Again, in his exhortation to servants in Ephesians, Paul called them to do the will of God from the heart. The appeal to the heart is an appeal to the core of the person's being. The Old Testament observation was that as a man thinks in his heart, so is he (Prov. 23:7). This does not indicate that Old Testament Jews believed the heart, rather than the brain, was the organ of thought. Rather, it was designed to indicate that there are actions that are superficial and motivated by external considerations, actions that lack devotion or passion, but what we think in our hearts is what we are truly committed to in the depth of our beings. The heart aspect of our thoughts is the controlling impulse of our lives. This is the impulse of *agape*, which reflects the love that has been shed abroad in our hearts. The Holy Spirit pierces the hearts of God's people in order to impel them to do the will of God.

Stauffer indicated that two chief forces work against an authentic expression of *agape*: mammon and vainglory. The heaping of riches motivated by a love of mammon cannot coexist with a love for God. This does not mean that prosperity clearly signals a lack of love for God, but it may be a danger signal for those who are blind to their own priorities. The rich man can enter the kingdom, but he does so with difficulty because of his vulnerability to the love of mammon (Mark 10:23–25).

Likewise, Jesus saw the vanity of those who seek the applause of men as a clear and present danger to the exercise of loving obedience. We see this in His sharp rebuke of the Pharisees:

> And as He spoke, a certain Pharisee asked Him to dine with him. So He went in and sat down to eat. When

the Pharisee saw it, he marveled that He had not first washed before dinner.

Then the Lord said to him, "Now you Pharisees make the outside of the cup and dish clean, but your inward part is full of greed and wickedness. Foolish ones! Did not He who made the outside make the inside also? But rather give alms of such things as you have; then indeed all things are clean to you.

"But woe to you Pharisees! For you tithe mint and rue and all manner of herbs, and pass by justice and the love of God. These you ought to have done, without leaving the others undone. Woe to you Pharisees! For you love the best seats in the synagogues and greetings in the marketplaces. Woe to you, scribes and Pharisees, hypocrites! For you are like graves which are not seen, and the men who walk over them are not aware of them." (Luke 11:37–44)

The Pharisees felt Jesus's sharp rebuke because they were hypocrites. The hypocrite in antiquity was an actor. His life was a pretense lived out on a stage before the gaze of men. It was lived for men and in front of men. The highest accolade for the hypocrite is human applause. Jesus said of His adversaries that they loved the best seats in the synagogues. The seats were not considered best merely because they afforded the best view of events but because they were positions of honor. But Jesus indicated that the love of prestige is incompatible with the love of God.

Stauffer mentioned a third threat to *agape* love: persecution, which can undermine a person's loving obedience to God. The avoidance of personal pain is a strong motivation for those with a weak and inconsistent love for God. Jesus warned His disciples:

> Behold, I send you out as sheep in the midst of wolves. Therefore be wise as serpents and harmless as doves. But beware of men, for they will deliver you up to councils and scourge you in their synagogues. You will be brought before governors and kings for My sake, as a testimony to them and to the Gentiles. But when they deliver you up, do not worry about how or what you should speak. For it will be given to you in that hour what you should speak; for it is not you who speak, but the Spirit of your Father who speaks in you.
>
> Now brother will deliver up brother to death, and a father his child; and children will rise up against parents and cause them to be put to death. And you will be hated by all for My name's sake. But he who endures to the end will be saved. When they persecute you in this city, flee to another. For assuredly, I say to you, you will not have gone through the cities of Israel before the Son of Man comes.
>
> A disciple is not above his teacher, nor a servant above his master. It is enough for a disciple that he be like his teacher, and a servant like his master. If they have called the master of the house Beelzebub, how much more will they call those of his household!

> Therefore do not fear them. For there is nothing cov-
> ered that will not be revealed, and hidden that will not
> be known. (Matt. 10:16–26)

Jesus did not want His disciples to be man-pleasers. He warned them to beware of men. This wariness was born of His certainty that His disciples would surely experience persecution in this world. To be a servant of Christ requires a willingness to participate in the sufferings of Christ. To flee from identification with His humiliation is to flee from participation in His exaltation. The servant is never above the master. If the master suffers, the servant suffers as well. If the master is hated, so his servant is despised. If the master is rejected by men and receives jeers rather than applause, so the scorn and derision of men ring in the ears of the servant.

Surely this is what Paul had in mind when he said, "I now rejoice in my sufferings for you, and fill up in my flesh what is lacking in the afflictions of Christ, for the sake of His body, which is the church" (Col. 1:24).

It is startling to hear Paul speak of something "lacking" in the afflictions of Christ, but he did not mean that there was some deficiency in the meritorious suffering of Christ that must be com-pensated for by our own afflictions. Since the merit of Christ is perfect, we cannot possibly add to it or subtract from it. The perfec-tion of His merit leaves no room for augmentation or diminution. The atoning work of Christ is finished. His sacrifice was offered once for all. Nevertheless, His body, the church, continues to participate in His suffering by way of identification with Him. In a narrow and restricted sense, the church is the continuing incarnation, but not in the sense that it is divine or that it redeems. It is the continuing incarnation in the sense that it remains His "body" in this world, giving visible testimony to His invisible reign as King of Kings.

Paul was able to rejoice in his sufferings because his heart was gripped by *agape*. His love for Christ necessitated also a love for His body, the church. Therefore, he could rejoice in his sufferings because those sufferings occurred while he was serving Christ by serving His church.

In this we see a remarkable contrast with Paul's initial encounter with the risen Christ, as recorded in the book of Acts:

> Then Saul, still breathing threats and murder against the disciples of the Lord, went to the high priest and asked letters from him to the synagogues of Damascus, so that if he found any who were of the Way, whether men or women, he might bring them bound to Jerusalem.
>
> As he journeyed he came near Damascus, and suddenly a light shone around him from heaven. Then he fell to the ground, and heard a voice saying to him, "Saul, Saul, why are you persecuting Me?"
>
> And he said, "Who are You, Lord?"
>
> Then the Lord said, "I am Jesus, whom you are persecuting. It is hard for you to kick against the goads."
>
> So he, trembling and astonished, said, "Lord, what do You want me to do?"
>
> Then the Lord said to him, "Arise and go into the city, and you will be told what you must do."

> And the men who journeyed with him stood
> speechless, hearing a voice but seeing no one. Then
> Saul arose from the ground, and when his eyes were
> opened he saw no one. But they led him by the hand
> and brought him into Damascus. And he was three
> days without sight, and neither ate nor drank. (9:1–9)

In this encounter, in which Paul was converted from an enemy of Christ who was breathing out fire against the church to a loving and devoted servant of Christ, Christ asked Paul why he was persecuting Him. Paul was not persecuting Jesus personally. He was attacking the church. But Jesus revealed that He considered attacks against His church to be attacks against Himself. The irony is that even before his conversion, Paul was already "filling up what was lacking in the sufferings of Christ" by afflicting the church rather than being afflicted.

The most fundamental demand Jesus imposed on His disciples was the demand to love God. But following the Old Testament, Jesus added to this command the command to love one's neighbor. Jesus was interrogated by His enemies on this point:

> But when the Pharisees heard that He had silenced the
> Sadducees, they gathered together. Then one of them,
> a lawyer, asked Him a question, testing Him, and say-
> ing, "Teacher, which is the great commandment in the
> law?"
>
> Jesus said to him, "'You shall love the LORD your
> God with all your heart, with all your soul, and with all

your mind.' This is the first and great commandment. And the second is like it: 'You shall love your neighbor as yourself.' On these two commandments hang all the Law and the Prophets." (Matt. 22:34–40)

The love of which Jesus spoke in this summary of the law is *agape*. Jesus would not allow the Pharisees to restrict the love of neighbor to one's compatriots, but showed that this obligation extends to all humanity. There was no room in Jesus's thinking for the notion of separation that sees redemption happening by means of keeping oneself at a safe distance from all impure people. Jesus challenged this idea of redemption by segregation throughout His entire public ministry. He made contact with publicans and sinners, dined with outcasts, and dialogued even with despised Samaritans such as the woman of Sychar (John 4).

Jesus's behavior, along with His teaching regarding love, prompted a lawyer to test Him with a provocative question:

> And behold, a certain lawyer stood up and tested Him, saying, "Teacher, what shall I do to inherit eternal life?"
>
> He said to him, "What is written in the law? What is your reading of it?"
>
> So he answered and said, "'You shall love the LORD your God with all your heart, with all your soul, with all your strength, and with all your mind,' and 'your neighbor as yourself.'"
>
> And He said to him, "You have answered rightly; do this and you will live."

> But he, wanting to justify himself, said to Jesus, "And who is my neighbor?" (Luke 10:25–29)

Luke noted that the lawyer's question was insincere. Perhaps he was trying to trip Jesus up by bringing His interpretation of the Old Testament law into conflict with rabbinic tradition. Driven by a motivation of self-justification, which could have originated only in a desire to escape the judgment of having failed to meet the law's requirements, the lawyer posed the question "Who is my neighbor?" The very question reveals that the man had assumed a restricted view of *neighbor,* believing that the term did not extend to the whole of humanity. It was this question that prompted Jesus to utter perhaps His best-known and most-loved parable, the parable of the good Samaritan:

> Then Jesus answered and said: "A certain man went down from Jerusalem to Jericho, and fell among thieves, who stripped him of his clothing, wounded him, and departed, leaving him half dead. Now by chance a certain priest came down that road. And when he saw him, he passed by on the other side. Likewise a Levite, when he arrived at the place, came and looked, and passed by on the other side. But a certain Samaritan, as he journeyed, came where he was. And when he saw him, he had compassion. So he went to him and bandaged his wounds, pouring on oil and wine; and he set him on his own animal, brought him to an inn, and took care of him. On the next day, when he departed,

he took out two denarii, gave them to the innkeeper, and said to him, 'Take care of him; and whatever more you spend, when I come again, I will repay you.' So which of these three do you think was neighbor to him who fell among the thieves?"

And he said, "He who showed mercy on him."

Then Jesus said to him, "Go and do likewise." (Luke 10:30–37)

Stauffer saw in this parable Jesus's radical smashing of the tradition that restricted the idea of the neighborhood to those close at hand or to members of an affinity group. Indeed, Jesus eschewed an abstract answer to the question "Who is my neighbor?" He offered no connotative definition. Instead, His reply was denotative; it came by way of a concrete example.

The players in the parable include the thieves, the victim, a priest, a Levite, a Samaritan, and an innkeeper. Of these characters, the priest, the Levite, and the Samaritan came into the closest contact with the victim in his time of need. That need was extreme. We are told that the thieves not only robbed the man but also stripped him of his clothes, wounded him, and left him "half dead."

While he was in this half-dead condition, the victim was approached by the priest, the Levite, and the Samaritan. Obviously Jesus chose these characters with care. Since both priests and Levites were set apart for a holy vocation, a vocation of ministry that included intercession and care for people, especially wounded people, Jesus created a sense of expectancy in His hearers that the first person on the scene, a priest, would stop to attend to the victim's needs. But he did not stop. Instead, he "passed by on the other side." We do not know whether he crossed the road in order to avoid the man or if he merely kept himself at a distance from the victim. We do know that the priest saw the man in the road and obviously recognized his extreme need. Jesus did not tell us why the priest passed by the miserable man. Perhaps he was frightened, in a hurry, or simply hard of heart, inured to the pain of others. In like manner, the Levite chose the other side of the road.

In stark contrast to these men of highly respected office in the caste system of the Jews, the third traveler was a Samaritan, the last person a Jew would consider his neighbor. Jesus described the response of the Samaritan in a series of actions.

The first response was compassion, which was immediate on seeing the severely wounded man. Jesus said, "When he saw him, he had compassion." The term *compassion* describes a feeling. While it is possible to feel sorry for people without doing anything concrete on their behalf, this Samaritan's compassion was not merely a feeling. His compassion resulted in action: he went to the man, he bandaged his wounds, he poured oil and wine on his wounds, he set him on his own animal, he brought him to an inn, and he took care of him. Further, Jesus told us that the Samaritan spent the night at the inn and then departed, leaving the man in the care of the innkeeper. The Samaritan also spent his own money to pay for the ongoing care of the man.

Jesus ended His story with a question: "So which of these three do you think was neighbor to him who fell among the thieves?" The lawyer at this point was a quick study. There was no way he could miss or duck the point of Jesus's parable. He replied: "He who showed mercy on him." Then Jesus said to him, "Go and do likewise."

It is important for us to see that in this parable, Jesus not only identified who is one's neighbor, but also gave vital information about the meaning of *agape*. The dispute was not simply over the issue of who is one's neighbor. It also included the question of what it means to love one's neighbor. Neither the priest nor the Levite displayed love toward his neighbor. They might have felt some concern for the man they passed by, but whatever they felt, it was not *agape*.

It is important to keep in mind that we are examining the meaning of *agape* as it applies to human relationships. But *agape* also defines the love of God Himself. The God of Scripture is revealed in the Old Testament drama of Exodus as a God who acts in response to hearing the cries of His people:

> And God spoke to Moses and said to him: "I am the LORD. I appeared to Abraham, to Isaac, and to Jacob, as God Almighty, but by My name LORD I was not known to them. I have also established My covenant with them, to give them the land of Canaan, the land of their pilgrimage, in which they were strangers. And I have also heard the groaning of the children of Israel whom the Egyptians keep in bondage, and I have remembered My covenant. Therefore say to the children of Israel: 'I am the LORD; I will bring you out from under the burdens of the Egyptians, I will rescue you from their bondage, and I will redeem you with an outstretched arm and with great judgments. I will take you as My people, and I will be your God. Then you shall know that I am the LORD your God who brings

you out from under the burdens of the Egyptians. And I will bring you into the land which I swore to give to Abraham, Isaac, and Jacob; and I will give it to you as a heritage: I am the LORD.'" (Exod. 6:2–8)

The love of God was manifest when He heard the groans of His people. He had compassion on them. He did not move to the other side of the road, but He acted out of compassionate love to rescue His people. God promised to do five things: to bring His people out from under the burdens of the Egyptians, to rescue them from bondage, to redeem them with an outstretched arm and with great judgments, to take them to be His people, and to be their God. In addition to these acts of rescue and liberation, God promised that He would bring the people to the Promised Land and that they would receive it as their heritage.

LOVE YOUR ENEMY

Jesus's radical demand to love extends beyond the love of God and the love of neighbor to include the love of one's enemies. This mandate is expressed in the Sermon on the Mount:

You have heard that it was said, "You shall love your neighbor and hate your enemy." But I say to you, love your enemies, bless those who curse you, do good to those who hate you, and pray for those who spitefully use you and persecute you, that you may be sons of your Father in heaven; for He makes His sun rise on the evil and on the good, and sends rain on the just and on the unjust. For if you love those who love you, what reward have you? Do not even the tax collectors do the same? And if you greet your brethren only, what do you do more than others? Do not even the tax collectors do so? Therefore you shall be perfect, just as your Father in heaven is perfect. (Matt. 5:43–48)

By referring to what His hearers had "heard … said," Jesus used an idiomatic expression that refers to the *Halakhah*, the oral tradition of the rabbis. This stands in bold contrast to the phrase "It is written …" Jesus did not criticize the written word of the Old Testament; rather, He criticized the traditions of the rabbis. They interpreted the Old Testament mandate to love one's neighbor as implying that it was appropriate to hate one's enemies. Jesus placed His words in contrast to and in conflict with this rabbinic oral tradition. After citing what the rabbis said, Jesus said, "But I say to you …"

With this command, Jesus gave content to what it means to love one's enemies. It includes blessing those who curse us, doing good to those who hate us, and praying for those who spitefully use us and persecute us. Jesus grounded this demand of *agape* love on the example of the Father's *agape* love for us. We are to behave in this manner in order to show that we are sons of our heavenly Father. He reminded His hearers of the benevolent and beneficent love of God for His own enemies. To love those who love us carries no great virtue or reward. Even the tax collectors do that, showing that there is honor among thieves.

Jesus made this demand of love for our enemies a part of the radical new situation He initiated with the breakthrough of the kingdom of God. *Agape* is to be a cardinal ingredient of the kingdom.

A fascinating discussion regarding the meaning of *agape* is found in Jesus's conversation with Simon Peter:

> So when they had eaten breakfast, Jesus said to Simon Peter, "Simon, son of Jonah, do you love Me more than these?"
>
> He said to Him, "Yes, Lord; You know that I love You."
>
> He said to him, "Feed My lambs."
>
> He said to him again a second time, "Simon, son of Jonah, do you love Me?"
>
> He said to Him, "Yes, Lord; You know that I love You."
>
> He said to him, "Tend My sheep."
>
> He said to him the third time, "Simon, son of Jonah, do you love Me?" Peter was grieved because He said to him the third time, "Do you love Me?"
>
> And he said to Him, "Lord, You know all things; You know that I love You."
>
> Jesus said to him, "Feed My sheep. Most assuredly, I say to you, when you were younger, you girded yourself and walked where you wished; but when you are old, you will stretch out your hands, and another will gird you and carry you where you do not wish." This He spoke, signifying by what death he would glorify

God. And when He had spoken this, He said to him,
"Follow Me." (John 21:15–19)

What is so intriguing about this interchange is the way in
which the word for "love" changes between *agape* and *philein*. When
Jesus posed His first question to Simon Peter—"Do you love Me
more than these?"—He used a form of *agape*. However, when Peter
answered the question by saying, "Yes, Lord; You know that I love
You," he used a form of the verb *philein*.

This switch of words has engendered much debate among commentators. Some have argued that there is no significance at all in
the use of two different words for love since *agape* and *philein* often
are used interchangeably in John's gospel. Others argue, however,
that there is significance in the switch of words. Jesus asked whether
Peter had *agape* love for Him, and Peter responded with a profession
of *philein* love. Perhaps this indicates that Peter was acknowledging,
especially in light of his threefold denial of Jesus, that his love for
Christ had not reached the level of *agape*.

With Peter's response, Jesus gave him a command: "Feed My
lambs." A consequence of love must be the nurture of those who
belong to Christ, those whom He regards as His lambs. As the
dialogue continued, Jesus again asked Peter if he loved Him. Again
Jesus referred to *agape* love in His question. Peter replied in the
same manner as his first answer, using the *philein* form of love. Jesus
responded by commanding that Peter tend His sheep. Jesus changed
the command from "feed" to "tend" and from "lambs" to "sheep."
Again, these vocabulary changes may be simply stylistic and have no
special significance. On the other hand, they may indicate a subtle

distinction between the care of young believers and more mature believers. The infant "lambs" require simple feeding, while the adults need not only feeding but also guidance, which requires greater skill.

When Jesus asked the third time whether Peter loved Him, He suddenly switched from *agape* to the lesser term *philein*, the term Peter had been using. This time the text says that Peter was grieved by this question. Was he grieved because Jesus pressed the issue for the third time? Was he grieved because the third question evoked memories of his threefold denial? Was he grieved because Jesus retreated to the use of *philein*? Was Jesus questioning not only whether Peter had reached the level of *agape* but even whether he had attained the level of *philein*? Peter protested that Jesus surely knew that he loved Him. Again Jesus gave the mandate: "Feed My sheep." Perhaps this indicates that even the mature sheep still require the nurture of spiritual food.

Whatever Jesus intended by this close interrogation of Simon Peter, one thing is certain: love requires taking care of the people of God. Those who stand in the Apostolic tradition and ministry must administer the love of Christ to all who are placed under their care.

Agape love is not only a nurturing love, as God nurtures His people and feeds them the heavenly bread; it is also a pardoning love. The pardon that God provides for His people is in and through the One the Father loves with *agape* love. It is in and through the work of the "Beloved" of the Father that pardon is extended.

Not only did *agape* take on a new dimension with the content Jesus gave to it, the Apostles further nuanced it in the early church. For Paul, the pouring of *agape* into our hearts (Rom. 5:5) is an event of critical importance in the life of the Christian. This gift of love makes it possible for the Christian to imitate Christ.

It is also *agape* love that Paul saw manifested in the divine work of election. Indeed, it may be said that the ultimate force of *agape* is seen in the determination of God that His elect be redeemed thoroughly. The efficacy of the work of Christ does not depend on the response of the believer. The efficacy is rooted in the ministry of Jesus Himself, who not only makes the salvation of His sheep possible, but also, by the perfection of His work, makes their salvation certain.

Finally, the fruit of *agape* in the life of the Christian is the creation of the new person in Christ. The new man or woman is the result of the divine craftsmanship that shapes and molds us into the image of Christ. It is by the power of *agape* that we are enabled to grow up into the fullness of Christ.

Of course, the most extensive exposition of the nature and behavior of *agape* is set forth in the famous "love chapter," 1 Corinthians 13. In the next chapter, we will examine that exposition so that we may not only deepen our understanding of what love requires of us, but also see how that love reveals the character of God.

CHAPTER 9

THE GREATEST OF
THESE ...

One of the favorite chapters of the New Testament among Christians is chapter 13 of 1 Corinthians. Popularly known as "the love chapter," it is frequently read during marriage ceremonies, and its words are borrowed to serve as lyrics for anthems and solos.

The popularity of this chapter reveals a tendency among believers to treat its content in a superficial or sentimental manner. However, a close look at this chapter should provoke us to a deep repentance, because it reveals what *agape* demands of us as we are called to be imitators of God. But as the demands of *agape* are spelled out for us, they reveal the nature of the love in the character of God Himself. When we measure our behavior against God's standard, it is clear that our behavior falls far short of what love requires. Normally we do not enjoy the exposure of our failures and sins, so perhaps we read this chapter through rose-colored glasses to shield ourselves from the indictment it delivers against us.

Another problem we encounter in examining this chapter is the tendency to rip it out of the immediate context of the epistle. The thirteenth chapter is not an independent study of the meaning of *agape*, but is a crucial section of the Apostolic argument concerning the nature of the church and the exercise of spiritual gifts (the *charismata*) within the church.

Chapter 12 concerns the manifestation of the Spirit of God in the life of the church in terms of His equipping members of the body of Christ with diverse gifts and ministries. Paul was concerned about the importance of all of the gifts as they serve to unify and edify the whole body. The goal is unity in diversity.

After laying the groundwork for this concern, Paul provided a transition from chapter 12 to chapter 13 by writing, "But earnestly desire the best gifts. And yet I show you a more excellent way" (12:31). The Apostle elaborated on this "more excellent way" in chapter 13:

> Though I speak with the tongues of men and of angels, but have not love, I have become sounding brass or a clanging cymbal. And though I have the gift of prophecy, and understand all mysteries and all knowledge, and though I have all faith, so that I could remove mountains, but have not love, I am nothing. And though I bestow all my goods to feed the poor, and though I give my body to be burned, but have not love, it profits me nothing.

Love suffers long and is kind; love does not envy; love does not parade itself, is not puffed up; does not behave rudely, does not seek its own, is not provoked, thinks no evil; does not rejoice in iniquity, but rejoices in the truth; bears all things, believes all things, hopes all things, endures all things.

Love never fails. But whether there are prophecies, they will fail; whether there are tongues, they will cease; whether there is knowledge, it will vanish away. For we know in part and we prophesy in part. But when that which is perfect has come, then that which is in part will be done away.

When I was a child, I spoke as a child, I understood as a child, I thought as a child; but when I became a man, I put away childish things. For now we see in a mirror, dimly, but then face to face. Now I know in part, but then I shall know just as I also am known.

And now abide faith, hope, love, these three; but the greatest of these is love.

In writing this chapter, I used commentaries on 1 Corinthians, as well as the insights of Jonathan Edwards set forth in his book *Charity and Its Fruits*. This book is one of the most important books I have ever read and one that I return to repeatedly in the course of my studies and ministry in the things of God. Edwards saw in 1 Corinthians 13 a powerful revelation of the nature of divine love. He made two observations.

First, all true Christian love is one and the same in its principle. It comes from the same source or fountain and is communicated to the believer by the same Holy Spirit. In this love, both God and man are loved from the same motive, namely, for holiness' sake.

Second, all virtue that is saving, or distinguishing of true Christians, is summed up in Christian love. It is love that disposes us to honor God as God, to adore and worship Him. Love recognizes God's right to govern us and His worthiness to be the object of our obedience. At the same time, love disposes us to treat our neighbors with honor and respect. We are not readily inclined to cheat, defraud, or otherwise work ill toward those we love. Indeed, the good works that are the fruit of saving faith are performed out of love. Faith works by love. Saving faith is not mere intellectual assent but includes a genuine affection for its object, making love the heart and soul of saving faith. All Christian holiness begins with faith in Christ.

Edwards listed seven ways in which 1 Corinthians 13 instructs us in the nature of true love. By way of summary they are as follows:

1. Love reveals the right Christian spirit.
2. Love reveals to those who profess faith whether their Christian experience is genuine.
3. Love reveals a friendly spirit, which spirit is the spirit of heaven.
4. Love shows the pleasantness of the Christian life.
5. Love reveals why strife and contention tend to the ruin of Christians.
6. Love reveals an urgent need to guard against envy,

malice, bitterness, and other such bad attitudes that overthrow the work of love.

7. Love calls us to love even the worst of our enemies, as it tempers the spirit of the Christian and is the sum of Christianity.

THE SUPREME IMPORTANCE OF LOVE

Let us turn our attention now to an examination of the text itself:

> Though I speak with the tongues of men and of angels, but have not love, I have become sounding brass or a clanging cymbal. (v. 1)

Paul introduced this chapter with a series of comparisons and contrasts designed to demonstrate the supreme importance of love above all other gifts. By no means did the Apostle despise the other gifts of the Spirit, especially the extraordinary manifestations of such gifts as tongues (*glossolalia*). Yet it is clear from the context of this epistle that the saints in Corinth were competing over the status and relative importance of their individual gifts. They exalted themselves because they displayed spectacular gifts such as tongues. Paul set the record straight by arguing that a display of such gifts, even if they transcend the human and reach the realm of angelic language, if it is without love, is only so much noise. The sound of brass and clanging cymbals is cacophony, not symphony. The presence of love is the *sine qua non* of the value of the other gifts. Its absence vitiates or empties the value of the gifts.

We live in a culture in which gifts and talents conceal or eclipse the destructive power of sin. We have an ultimate double standard of morality for the talented and the powerful. If a movie star is talented and entertaining on the silver screen, it does not matter that he or she has been through multiple stormy marriages and divorces. If a professional athlete excels on the field, his personal behavior is excusable. A president of the United States may be excused for gross immorality and even for perjury and obstruction of justice because, during his term, the economy prospered. In modern culture, clanging cymbals mean more than the works of love.

> And though I have the gift of prophecy, and under-
> stand all mysteries and all knowledge, and though I
> have all faith, so that I could remove mountains, but
> have not love, I am nothing. (v. 2)

In chapter 14, Paul commended the pursuit of spiritual gifts to the Corinthians, giving special attention to the gift of prophecy. It is seen as superior to tongues because the one who prophesies edifies, exhorts, and comforts others. A few verses later, Paul said, "I wish you all spoke with tongues, but even more that you prophesied; for he who prophesies is greater than he who speaks with tongues, unless indeed he interprets, that the church may receive edification" (v. 5).

However, in chapter 13, Paul declared that if the extraordinary or miraculous gifts of prophecy and knowledge are manifested without love, those who exercise them are nothing. In themselves, these gifts have great value, but that value is reduced to zero when love is absent. The application is to the church, where those who are talented in preaching and teaching are held in high esteem, but the esteem is misplaced if these gifts are exercised without *agape*.

> And though I bestow all my goods to feed the poor,
> and though I give my body to be burned, but have not
> love, it profits me nothing. (v. 3)

It may be hard to imagine someone giving all of his or her property to the poor without being motivated by love. It is even more difficult to imagine someone sacrificing his or her life by volunteering to be burned at the stake without love. Yet such things are indeed possible. People may give away their goods out of pride or in an attempt to win the applause of others for their "charity." It is possible to be charitable without possessing the essence of charity in one's heart. Generous donors often receive the flattery of people. They are fawned over with deference because their gifts are so helpful. The recognition that comes with charitable giving can easily feed the pride of the flesh. The easiest way to get appointments with busy and prominent people is to invite them to ceremonies in which they will be honored. We are rarely too busy to receive accolades from others. Buildings are named after donors of large gifts, and money may easily be exchanged for fame. But such an investment of our capital without the accompaniment of love yields a net profit of zero.

Edwards, in some of his other works, spoke of acts that appear good on the surface but may be motivated by what he called "enlightened self-interest." A deed may appear to be sacrificial while its real motive is masked to human observers. But the divine vision can penetrate the mask and see the motivation of the heart.

Paul's warning about works without love reiterates the warning Jesus gave in the Sermon on the Mount: "Not everyone who says to Me, 'Lord, Lord,' shall enter the kingdom of heaven, but he who does the will of My Father in heaven. Many will say to Me in that day, 'Lord, Lord, have we not prophesied in Your name, cast out demons in Your name, and done many wonders in Your name?' And then I will declare to them, 'I never knew you; depart from Me, you who practice lawlessness!'" (Matt. 7:21–23).

Jesus was speaking of people who will claim to know Him intimately at the last judgment. They will point to their extraordinary deeds of talent and valor. Their dossiers will include references to prophesying, casting out demons, and performing wonders. Yet Jesus will declare that He not only does not know them but that He *never* knew them. Then He will command them to leave His presence, to depart from Him. The reason He will give for this judicial dismissal will be that they practiced lawlessness. To be lawless is to be without any genuine love for God. The heart that possesses *agape* cannot be lawless. The presence of lawlessness signals the absence of *agape*.

After establishing the supreme importance of love as a necessary condition for the value of the exercise of other gifts, Paul proceeded to give his exposition of the nature of *agape*.

LOVE SUFFERS LONG AND IS KIND

In verse 4, Paul began to make a series of affirmations about love. He wrote:

> Love suffers long and is kind. (v. 4a)

Already we see the correlation between how the Christian is commanded to behave and the customary behavior of God Himself. Just as God is the ultimate standard of love, so He is the ultimate standard of long-suffering. It is noteworthy that here long-suffering is seen as a characteristic of love, while in Galatians it is mentioned as a fruit of the Spirit distinct from the fruit of love (5:22).

One of the most difficult virtues for us is to patiently bear injuries from others. When we are called on to suffer, it is our earnest hope and prayer that the suffering will be short. Protracted suffering is the most difficult to bear. We think of those whom Jesus healed who had suffered from their maladies for many years, such as the man born blind, the woman with the issue of blood, and the crippled man by the pool of Bethesda:

> After this there was a feast of the Jews, and Jesus went up to Jerusalem. Now there is in Jerusalem by the Sheep Gate a pool, which is called in Hebrew, Bethesda, having five porches. In these lay a great multitude of sick people, blind, lame, paralyzed, waiting for the moving of the water. For an angel went down at a certain time into the pool and stirred up the water; then whoever

stepped in first, after the stirring of the water, was made well of whatever disease he had. Now a certain man was there who had an infirmity thirty-eight years. When Jesus saw him lying there, and knew that he already had been in that condition a long time, He said to him, "Do you want to be made well?"

The sick man answered Him, "Sir, I have no man to put me into the pool when the water is stirred up; but while I am coming, another steps down before me."

Jesus said to him, "Rise, take up your bed and walk." And immediately the man was made well, took up his bed, and walked. (John 5:1–9)

This poor man had been paralyzed for thirty-eight years. For almost four decades, he had nourished hope that he would gain some relief from his affliction. The end of his pain came when he encountered Jesus. The healing of Christ was the prize of his long-suffering.

With physical injury or disease, we have no choice but to suffer as long as the malady lasts. When it comes to bearing the personal attacks or slander of others, our behavior takes on a much greater voluntary dimension. We may receive injuries at the hands of others that are physical or involve the loss of personal property. But the theft of our good name or the loss of our reputation by way of slander is difficult to accept. Edwards spoke of this:

> Some injure others in their good name, by
> reproaching or speaking evil of them behind their
> backs. No injury is more common, and no iniquity

more frequent or base than this. Other ways of injury are abundant; but the amount of injury by evil-speaking of this kind, is beyond account. Some injure others by making or spreading false reports about them, and so cruelly slandering them. Others, without saying that which is directly false, greatly misrepresent things, picturing out everything respecting their neighbors in the worst colors, exaggerating their faults, and setting them forth as far greater than they really are, always speaking of them in an unfair and unjust manner. A great deal of injury is done among neighbors by thus uncharitably judging one another, and putting injurious and evil constructions on one another's words and actions.[1]

To bear slander, insults, and harsh criticism requires an extraordinary measure of love. We are quick to lash out and retaliate in kind against those who abuse us. Our suffering threshold is low. We must look to Christ Himself as the perfect model of long-suffering in the face of such abuse.

In the first place, we must recognize that much of the criticism we receive, though painful, is not slander because we richly deserve it. Such was not true of Christ. Every criticism leveled against Him was slanderous because He was sinless. The attacks on His character had no legitimate foundation in fact. Throughout His ministry, He was subjected to false charges. Certainly no person in history was more libeled than was Jesus, yet He was willing to lose His reputation for the benefit of His people. He suffered frequently in silence as His enemies did everything in their power to destroy His good name.

This suffering was foreshadowed in Isaiah: "He was oppressed and He was afflicted, yet He opened not His mouth; He was led as a lamb to the slaughter, and as a sheep before its shearers is silent, so He opened not His mouth" (53:7). In this regard Jesus not only displayed a perfect human example of long-suffering, but also modeled for us the long-suffering of God.

Paul added to the notion of long-suffering the quality of kindness. The long-suffering of *agape* is a kind long-suffering. Again we see a quality added to love that is elsewhere distinguished from love. Just as long-suffering is distinguished as a fruit of the Spirit, so is kindness (Gal. 5:22). But here kindness modifies love rather than standing alone as a separate virtue.

When Jesus commanded His people to love their enemies, He appealed to the love of God as the ultimate example of One who is kind toward those who are ungrateful and evil:

> And just as you want men to do to you, you also do to them likewise.
>
> But if you love those who love you, what credit is that to you? For even sinners love those who love them. And if you do good to those who do good to you, what credit is that to you? For even sinners do the same. And if you lend to those from whom you hope to receive back, what credit is that to you? For even sinners lend to sinners to receive as much back. But love your enemies, do good, and lend, hoping for

nothing in return; and your reward will be great, and you will be sons of the Most High. For He is kind to the unthankful and evil. Therefore be merciful, just as your Father also is merciful. (Luke 6:31–36)

The kindness of which Jesus spoke is related to the practical application of the Golden Rule. To be kind toward others is merely doing to them what we would like them to do to us. This kindness is linked to mercy. We have already seen that God's love is manifested by and through His mercy. Mercy is an act of kindness. It is also an expression of tenderness.

David appealed to the tender mercy of God in his penitential prayer (Ps. 51:1). The opposite of kindness or tender mercy is the destructive attitude of mean-spiritedness. The mean person takes pleasure in harming or injuring people. He or she enjoys other people's pain. Though God Himself punishes the wicked, He takes no delight in their pain. It is one thing to be firm in applying justice; it is another to be cruel or mean.

If we examine the behavior of Jesus as He dealt with people during His public ministry, certain traits become evident. On the one hand, He was consistent with the description of the Messiah presented by the prophet Isaiah, as quoted by Matthew:

But when Jesus knew it, He withdrew from there. And great multitudes followed Him, and He healed them all. Yet He warned them not to make Him known, that it might be fulfilled which was spoken by Isaiah the prophet, saying:

"Behold! My Servant whom I have chosen,

My Beloved in whom My soul is well pleased!

I will put My Spirit upon Him,

And He will declare justice to the Gentiles.

He will not quarrel nor cry out,

Nor will anyone hear His voice in the streets.

A bruised reed He will not break,

And smoking flax He will not quench,

Till He sends forth justice to victory;

And in His name Gentiles will trust." (12:15–21)

Jesus was careful never to break or crush the bruised reed. If we look at the way He treated the poor and oppressed, the infirm and the wayward, we quickly see this tender spirit at work. His kindness to the woman at the well (John 4:5–26) and even toward the woman caught in adultery (John 7:53–8:11) displayed this attitude.

On the other hand, when we see Jesus with the scribes and the Pharisees, we see a firmness and strength that is not so tender. He was not mean spirited, though the Pharisees imagined Him so in light of the strong words He used to rebuke them. To call people vipers, blind guides, whitewashed tombs, and children of the Devil is not normally viewed as an exercise in tenderness (Matt. 12:34; 23:16, 27, 33; John 8:44). Jesus's pattern was clear: With the weak He was exceedingly tender. With the strong and powerful, He asked no quarter and gave none. This "double standard" was based on the responsibility that those in positions of power carried. With the religious leaders' higher responsibility came a requisite culpability for injuring the lambs under their power and care. To the proud and arrogant, God is not always merciful. He will take down the mighty from their seats. This contrast of treatment is vividly expressed by the virgin Mary in the Magnificat:

And Mary said:

> "My soul magnifies the Lord,
> And my spirit has rejoiced in God my Savior.
> For He has regarded the lowly state of His maidservant;
> For behold, henceforth all generations will call me blessed.
> For He who is mighty has done great things for me,
> And holy is His name.
> And His mercy is on those who fear Him
> From generation to generation.
> He has shown strength with His arm;
> He has scattered the proud in the imagination of their hearts.
> He has put down the mighty from their thrones,
> And exalted the lowly.
> He has filled the hungry with good things,
> And the rich He has sent away empty.
> He has helped His servant Israel,
> In remembrance of His mercy,
> As He spoke to our fathers,
> To Abraham and to his seed forever." (Luke 1:46–55)

The contrast is between God's strength and His tender mercy. The Lord is both tough and tender, just and merciful. He exalts the lowly and scatters the proud.

NOT ENVIOUS, BOASTFUL, OR PROUD

Paul went on to say:

> Love does not envy; love does not parade itself, is not puffed up. (v. 4b)

The character of *agape* shows no envy. Here Paul detailed what love is not. Envy is a violation of the tenth commandment, which prohibits the sin of coveting. It is out of envy that people are moved to do violence to their neighbors. Envy is the root of theft, murder, slander, and a host of other crimes against humanity. The motive for the treachery Joseph's brothers committed against him was envy:

> Now Israel loved Joseph more than all his children, because he was the son of his old age. Also he made him a tunic of many colors. But when his brothers saw that their father loved him more than all his brothers, they hated him and could not speak peaceably to him.
>
> Now Joseph had a dream, and he told it to his brothers; and they hated him even more. So he said to them, "Please hear this dream which I have dreamed: There we were, binding sheaves in the field. Then behold, my sheaf arose and also stood upright; and indeed your sheaves stood all around and bowed down to my sheaf."
>
> And his brothers said to him, "Shall you indeed reign over us? Or shall you indeed have dominion over

us?" So they hated him even more for his dreams and for his words.

Then he dreamed still another dream and told it to his brothers, and said, "Look, I have dreamed another dream. And this time, the sun, the moon, and the eleven stars bowed down to me."

So he told it to his father and his brothers; and his father rebuked him and said to him, "What is this dream that you have dreamed? Shall your mother and I and your brothers indeed come to bow down to the earth before you?" And his brothers envied him, but his father kept the matter in mind. (Gen. 37:3–11)

The envy of the brothers that prompted them to sell Joseph into slavery was rooted in their hatred of him. Envy and hate go together. Envy and love are incompatible.

The envy that was manifest in the actions of Joseph's brothers was also evident in actions taken against Christ: "Now at the feast the governor was accustomed to releasing to the multitude one prisoner whom they wished. And at that time they had a notorious prisoner called Barabbas. Therefore, when they had gathered together, Pilate said to them, 'Whom do you want me to release to you? Barabbas, or Jesus who is called Christ?' For he knew that they had handed Him over because of envy" (Matt. 27:15–18).

In our society cultural analysts speak of the "politics of envy," where politicians, for their own interests, stir up strife among people to create a kind of class warfare. The poor are set against the rich, employees against employers, women against men. Envy is the breeding ground for strife and even war. Envy is not restricted to the poor. The wealthy often have an insatiable lust for greater riches, so that the man who owns one yacht boils in envy against the man who owns two.

An axiom of modern pagan culture is "If you've got it, flaunt it." Those who have wealth and/or power can easily provoke envy by their ostentatious display of their possessions and positions. This was a favorite trick of the Pharisees, who liked to parade their signs of honor:

> Then Jesus spoke to the multitudes and to His disciples, saying: "The scribes and the Pharisees sit in Moses' seat. Therefore whatever they tell you to observe, that observe and do, but do not do according to their works; for they say, and do not do. For they bind heavy burdens, hard to bear, and lay them on men's shoulders; but they themselves will not move them with one of their fingers. But all their works they do to be seen by men. They make their phylacteries broad and enlarge the borders of their garments. They love the best places at feasts, the best seats in the synagogues, greetings in the marketplaces, and to be called by men, 'Rabbi, Rabbi.' But you, do not be called 'Rabbi'; for One is your Teacher, the Christ, and you are all brethren." (Matt. 23:1–8)

Paul also said that "love does not parade itself, is not puffed up." Parading of oneself is a mark of pride. The expression "proud as a peacock" describes the manner in which the peacock fans his multicolored tail feathers and displays them as he struts. The same phenomenon is exhibited among wild turkeys. During the mating season, when the male gobbler tries to entice a hen, he not only struts, but also fans his tail feathers and "puffs" himself up to appear much larger than normal.

Earlier in his first epistle to the Corinthians, Paul warned against the kind of knowledge that puffs up and contrasted it with love: "Now concerning things offered to idols: We know that we all have knowledge. Knowledge puffs up, but love edifies. And if anyone thinks that he knows anything, he knows nothing yet as he ought to know. But if anyone loves God, this one is known by Him" (8:1–3). Knowledge without love breeds arrogance. Knowledge, like riches, can be paraded for the applause of men. Such knowledge parades about without its more modest partner, wisdom.

By contrast, the mark of authentic love is humility. Humility does not know how to strut.

The humility of love relates first to God. When saints in Scripture referred to themselves as worms or dogs, they were not indulging in false modesty but were viewing themselves in the light of the distance in glory between themselves and their Creator. Consider Job's response after God spoke to him and unveiled His glory:

Moreover the LORD answered Job, and said:

"Shall the one who contends with the Almighty correct
Him?
He who rebukes God, let him answer it."

Then Job answered the LORD and said:

> "Behold, I am vile;
> What shall I answer You?
> I lay my hand over my mouth.
> Once I have spoken, but I will not answer;
> Yes, twice, but I will proceed no further." (Job 40:1–5)

When Job saw himself against the backdrop of the omnipotent God, he declared himself to be vile. But his self-abasement reached an even greater dimension after God's further self-disclosure:

> Then Job answered the LORD and said:
>
> "I know that You can do everything,
> And that no purpose of Yours can be withheld from You.
> You asked, 'Who is this who hides counsel without
>   knowledge?'
> Therefore I have uttered what I did not understand,
> Things too wonderful for me, which I did not know.
> Listen, please, and let me speak;
> You said, 'I will question you, and you shall answer Me.'
>
> "I have heard of You by the hearing of the ear,
> But now my eye sees You.
> Therefore I abhor myself,
> And repent in dust and ashes." (42:1–6)

This type of self-abasement runs counter to the cult of self-esteem and narcissism that defines our age. We fear that humility will destroy our confidence and good self-image. But our self-image is to be a reflection of the image of God. Sin has so tarnished that image that when we look to the standard, God's character, we are driven to humility.

But the humility of love relates not only to our view of ourselves in contrast to God; it also touches our view of ourselves with respect to other people. We are admonished to have a sober evaluation of ourselves: "For I say, through the grace given to me, to everyone who is among you, not to think of himself more highly than he ought to think, but to think soberly, as God has dealt to each one a measure of faith. For as we have many members in one body, but all the members do not have the same function, so we, being many, are one body in Christ, and individually members of one another" (Rom. 12:3–5).

In the context of the church we are to display a love that prefers others to ourselves. This is one of the most difficult, yet important, demands of *agape*.

NOT RUDE OR SELFISH

Continuing to catalog the aspects of *agape*, Paul wrote:

[Love] does not behave rudely, does not seek its own. (v. 5a)

A loving person is a polite person. We can see etiquette as being grounded in mere social custom or convention, or we can see it as being grounded in the higher principle of love. The word *courtesy* has its origins in the British system of monarchy, in which honor was seen as a supreme virtue. *Courtesy* is an abbreviated term for "court etiquette." It has to do with manners. In a conference address, Dr. Sinclair Ferguson, the Scottish theologian, related an anecdote in which the young Princess Elizabeth and her sister, Princess Margaret, were going to an official function. The Queen Mother warned them as they were ready to depart, "Remember, girls, *royal* manners."

Manners worthy of royalty are required of sons and daughters of the King. Those who possess *agape* love for God and His anointed King are called to polite behavior. To avoid rudeness means that we are not pushy, selfish, or coarse in our speech. Love does not express itself in gross language or actions.

The Apostle Peter also called Christians to be courteous as a manifestation of love: "Finally, all of you be of one mind, having compassion for one another; love as brothers, be tenderhearted, be courteous; not returning evil for evil or reviling for reviling, but on the contrary blessing, knowing that you were called to this, that you may inherit a blessing" (1 Pet. 3:8–9). Here Peter linked courtesy to compassion, love, and tenderheartedness.

Harshness of speech and demeanor is a form of rudeness. When we interrupt each other in conversation, we reveal a kind of self-ishness that is inherent in rudeness. When Paul was on trial before King Agrippa, he was granted permission to present his defense. Yet while Paul was recounting his conversion experience on the road to Damascus, he was interrupted by Festus:

> Now as he thus made his defense, Festus said with a loud voice, "Paul, you are beside yourself! Much learn-ing is driving you mad!"

But he said, "I am not mad, most noble Festus, but speak the words of truth and reason. For the king, before whom I also speak freely, knows these things; for I am convinced that none of these things escapes his attention, since this thing was not done in a corner. King Agrippa, do you believe the prophets? I know that you do believe."

Then Agrippa said to Paul, "You almost persuade me to become a Christian."

And Paul said, "I would to God that not only you, but also all who hear me today, might become both almost and altogether such as I am, except for these chains." (Acts 26:24–29)

When Paul was rudely interrupted and accused of being crazy, he maintained his composure and answered rudeness with politeness. Even in this context of being rudely insulted by his enemy, Paul exhibited the courtesy of *agape*.

Paul's declaration that love "does not seek its own" pierces the heart of every person. At the root of our sin lies the spirit of selfishness by which we seek our interests over the interests of others. We want to do it "our way." To seek the good of others and their welfare in acts of charity may not be too difficult if the good of others does not conflict with my own good. It is when there is a conflict between their good and my good that a supernatural love is needed.

The story of the competing mothers who came to Solomon for judgment illustrates the problem of the conflict of wills:

Now two women who were harlots came to the king, and stood before him. And one woman said, "O my lord, this woman and I dwell in the same house; and I gave birth while she was in the house. Then it happened, the third day after I had given birth, that this woman also gave birth. And we were together; no one was with us in the house, except the two of us in the house. And this woman's son died in the night, because she lay on him. So she arose in the middle of the night and took my son from my side, while your maidservant slept, and laid him in her bosom, and laid her dead child in my bosom. And when I rose in the morning to nurse my son, there he was, dead. But when I had examined him in the morning, indeed, he was not my son whom I had borne."

Then the other woman said, "No! But the living one is my son, and the dead one is your son."

And the first woman said, "No! But the dead one is your son, and the living one is my son."

Thus they spoke before the king.

And the king said, "The one says, 'This is my son, who lives, and your son is the dead one'; and the other says, 'No! But your son is the dead one, and my son is the living one.'" Then the king said, "Bring me a sword." So they brought a sword before the king. And the king said, "Divide the living child in two, and give half to one, and half to the other."

Then the woman whose son was living spoke to the king, for she yearned with compassion for her son;

and she said, "O my lord, give her the living child, and by no means kill him!"

But the other said, "Let him be neither mine nor yours, but divide him."

So the king answered and said, "Give the first woman the living child, and by no means kill him; she is his mother." (1 Kings 3:16–27)

This episode does far more than illustrate the gift of wisdom God had granted to Solomon. It reveals a quality of love. In this case, the real mother of the baby was not motivated to give up her child out of love for the woman whose child was dead. Her motive was to save the life of her baby, whom she loved. The woman whose child was dead was so selfish that she would have preferred the baby be killed rather than have her rival possess the child who was rightfully hers. With this woman, selfishness knew no bounds.

Paul elsewhere commanded the exercise of unselfish love: "Therefore if there is any consolation in Christ, if any comfort of love, if any fellowship of the Spirit, if any affection and mercy, fulfill my joy by being like-minded, having the same love, being of one accord, of one mind. Let nothing be done through selfish ambition or conceit, but in lowliness of mind let each esteem others better than himself. Let each of you look out not only for his own interests, but also for the interests of others" (Phil. 2:1–4).

There is nothing wrong with looking after one's own interests. Seeking our own, in itself, is not sinful. In the incident before Solomon, the true mother's desire to claim her baby was not an expression of selfishness. She had the moral right to her baby. The love that seeks not its own is a love that seeks not its own exclusively or to the detriment of the rights of others. Paul showed us this in Philippians when he told us to have in mind the interests of others.

Unselfish love is linked to humility. Selfish love is a consequence of pride. It is not by accident that Paul's injunction to look out for the interests of others serves to introduce the famous "Kenotic hymn," a passage we examined earlier.

> Let this mind be in you which was also in Christ Jesus, who, being in the form of God, did not consider it robbery to be equal with God, but made Himself of no reputation, taking the form of a bondservant, and coming in the likeness of men. And being found in appearance as a man, He humbled Himself and became obedient to the point of death, even the death of the cross. Therefore God also has highly exalted Him and given Him the name which is above every name, that at the name of Jesus every knee should bow, of those in heaven, and of those on earth, and of those under the earth, and that every tongue should confess that Jesus Christ is Lord, to the glory of God the Father. (Phil. 2:5–11)

Paul called us to have the mind of Christ, by which He did not cling to His prerogatives of glory but was willing to lose His reputation for the sake of the redeemed. His self-humiliation was the supreme act of a love that did not seek its own.

IS NOT PROVOKED

The Bible does not forbid anger and does not view anger as inherently evil. God Himself manifests wrath, and Jesus openly expressed His indignation when He cleansed the temple:

> Now the Passover of the Jews was at hand, and Jesus went up to Jerusalem. And He found in the temple those who sold oxen and sheep and doves, and the money changers doing business. When He had made a whip of cords, He drove them all out of the temple, with the sheep and the oxen, and poured out the changers' money and overturned the tables. And He said to those who sold doves, "Take these things away! Do not make My Father's house a house of merchandise!" Then His disciples remembered that it was written, "Zeal for Your house has eaten Me up." (John 2:13–17)

Paul exhorted the Ephesians: "'Be angry, and do not sin': do not let the sun go down on your wrath, nor give place to the devil" (4:26–27). So anger can be appropriate at times.

However, it is a dangerous emotion that can explode into uncontrolled rage or simmer into a festering bitterness. God, in His love, is described as being slow to anger. He is not always on the edge of an uncontrolled rage. The love that is not provoked is a love that triumphs over an angry disposition. There are people who always seem to be angry about something and who wear their anger on their sleeves as a distorted badge of honor, but love is not like this. Love is not hotheaded. Its anger is not unsuitable.

Edwards noted four ways in which anger can be undue or unsuitable: in its nature, its occasion, its end, and its measure.[2]

The nature of anger may involve the opposition of a person's spirit to evil. But not all opposition to evil is necessarily anger. A person may have a calm and reasoned judgment that something is wrong and may oppose it without flying into a rage. Anger is undue when it contains ill will or a desire for vengeance.

Anger may be unchristian with respect to its occasion, as when anger is expressed without any just cause. Psychologists speak of situational anger, whereby a situation over which we have no control, such as rain ruining our picnic, provokes anger. The frustration that is provoked by the disappointment may cause people to be irritable with each other as anger seeks some object on which to vent.

The story of Jonah reveals unsuitable anger:

> But it displeased Jonah exceedingly, and he became angry. So he prayed to the LORD, and said, "Ah, LORD, was not this what I said when I was still in my country? Therefore I fled previously to Tarshish; for I know that You are a gracious and merciful God, slow to anger and abundant in lovingkindness, One who relents from doing harm. Therefore now, O LORD, please take my life from me, for it is better for me to die than to live!"
>
> Then the LORD said, "Is it right for you to be angry?"

So Jonah went out of the city and sat on the east side of the city. There he made himself a shelter and sat under it in the shade, till he might see what would become of the city. And the LORD God prepared a plant and made it come up over Jonah, that it might be shade for his head to deliver him from his misery. So Jonah was very grateful for the plant. But as morning dawned the next day God prepared a worm, and it so damaged the plant that it withered. And it happened, when the sun arose, that God prepared a vehement east wind; and the sun beat on Jonah's head, so that he grew faint. Then he wished death for himself, and said, "It is better for me to die than to live."

Then God said to Jonah, "Is it right for you to be angry about the plant?"

And he said, "It is right for me to be angry, even to death!"

But the LORD said, "You have had pity on the plant for which you have not labored, nor made it grow, which came up in a night and perished in a night." (Jon. 4:1–10)

Jonah's anger was misplaced. He was angry about the wrong things. In fact, he was angry with God without just cause. Rather than being irate, he should have been praising God for His mercy toward Nineveh.

Another occasion in which anger may be wrong is when people become upset over trivial matters. Here we violate the love that is to cover a multitude of sins (1 Pet. 4:8). Our "peeves" need not be domesticated to the point that we cherish them as pets.

Edwards's third way of identifying how anger can be evil is with respect to its end. Sinful anger is anger that has no godly purpose. It is a rash anger that seeks the mere gratification of our own pride.

Finally, Edwards spoke of undue anger, anger that is disproportionate to its cause. The anger is at a higher level or degree than its cause, or it may be undue in its duration. Paul had this in mind when he warned us not to let the sun go down on our wrath (Eph. 4:26). When the sun sets on our wrath, the wrath will likely persist and become bitterness or a grudge.

THINKS NO EVIL

Paul also said that love "thinks no evil." Love is not like the monkeys who see no evil, hear no evil, and speak no evil. To think no evil is not to view the world with rose-colored glasses or to retreat into a naive cocoon where evil thoughts cannot penetrate. Rather, to think no evil means to be ready to grant others the judgment of charity. We do not know what people's motives may be when they offend us or otherwise harm us. We can evaluate their actions in different ways. For example, we can judge them according to a best-case scenario or a worst-case scenario. Another option may be sober realism that falls between the best case and the worst case.

If someone approaches me with a gun in his hand and demands that I give him my money, I might reason afterward that he really did not mean to rob me. That would go beyond a best-case judgment of charity. The judgment of charity is due our neighbors when, in fact, we do not know why they did what they did or said what they said. To impugn their motives by assigning the worst possible causes to them would be to fail in love. It is rare indeed that people who wound us have acted with as much malice aforethought as we sometimes presume. Sometimes we want to think the worst of their motives so that we can justify our own feelings of vengeance.

Our problem is that we tend to reserve best-case judgments for our own motives. We are quick to grant the judgment of charity to ourselves while withholding it from others. A righteous judge is required to hear all the evidence before he renders a verdict. His judgment must be sober. If there is concrete evidence for malice aforethought, he must withhold a best-case evaluation. If there are mitigating circumstances, he must avoid the worst-case judgment. Love is not quick to think evil of others but demonstrates a forbearing spirit.

REJOICES NOT IN SIN BUT IN THE TRUTH

Paul went on to say:

> [Love] does not rejoice in iniquity, but rejoices in the
> truth. (v. 6)

One cannot love God and rejoice in evil, because evil opposes all that God is. Yet our fallen nature does precisely that. By nature we are at enmity with God and join in the satanic assault on His reign over us. Sin itself involves a love for and pleasure in evil. Sadly, we often seek our joy in sin. This is Paul's summary in his letter to the Romans:

> And even as they did not like to retain God in their knowledge, God gave them over to a debased mind, to do those things which are not fitting; being filled with all unrighteousness, sexual immorality, wickedness, covetousness, maliciousness; full of envy, murder, strife, deceit, evil-mindedness; they are whisperers, backbiters, haters of God, violent, proud, boasters, inventors of evil things, disobedient to parents, undiscerning, untrustworthy, unloving, unforgiving, unmerciful; who, knowing the righteous judgment of God, that those who practice such things are deserving of death, not only do the same but also approve of those who practice them. (1:28–32)

This list of vices includes not only those crimes committed by hardened criminals but also those acts common to fallen humanity. The depth of human depravity is seen in two ways. First, we do these things knowing that God so despises them that He declares them worthy of death. Second, and far worse, we approve of those who practice them.

If misery loves company, even more so does sin. By persuading others to participate in our sins, we make a statement that the sin is not really evil because others are doing it as well. This describes the modern culture, wherein practitioners of abortion, fornication, and homosexual acts not only seek permission but also demand that others approve of their deeds. This is not mere sinfulness; it is militant sinfulness that rejoices in evil.

Those who practice these gross evils are enraged if anyone tries to rain disapproval on their parade. They protest that Christians who oppose abortion and illicit sexual behavior are "unloving." However, God declares that rejoicing in these acts is what is opposed to true love. On the other hand, true love rejoices in the practice of righteousness. This joy is not the smug elation of prideful accomplishment but the joy of seeing the holiness of God honored.

Again it is important to note that taking pleasure and joy in sin is natural to our fallen humanity and that conversion does not instantly eradicate that inclination. Believers can also fall into the trap of seeking comrades to join them in their vices so that the voice of conscience may be muffled.

Love rejoices when righteousness triumphs. It does not cheer when the villain wins. There are no antiheroes where love prevails.

Contrary to rejoicing in evil, love rejoices in the truth. In this we see the inseparable link between love and truth. God is not only the ground of love but also the ground of truth. Jesus Himself is the truth. We cannot love Him and at the same time despise the truth or consider truth of no great significance.

During His trial before Pontius Pilate, Jesus engaged in a discussion about truth:

> Then Pilate entered the Praetorium again, called Jesus, and said to Him, "Are You the King of the Jews?"
>
> Jesus answered him, "Are you speaking for yourself about this, or did others tell you this concerning Me?"

Pilate answered, "Am I a Jew? Your own nation and the chief priests have delivered You to me. What have You done?"

Jesus answered, "My kingdom is not of this world. If My kingdom were of this world, My servants would fight, so that I should not be delivered to the Jews; but now My kingdom is not from here."

Pilate therefore said to Him, "Are You a king then?"

Jesus answered, "You say rightly that I am a king. For this cause I was born, and for this cause I have come into the world, that I should bear witness to the truth. Everyone who is of the truth hears My voice."

Pilate said to Him, "What is truth?" And when he had said this, he went out again to the Jews, and said to them, "I find no fault in Him at all." (John 18:33–38)

It is striking that the reason Jesus gave for His incarnation was to bear witness to the truth. This was well beyond the mind of Pilate, who obviously had no idea of what Jesus was speaking. Jesus gave other reasons for coming to this planet, such as to seek and to save those who were lost (Luke 19:10) and to give us abundant life (John 10:10). But these expressions are consistent with His assertion that He came to bear witness to the truth. It was His own commitment to truth that prodded Him to fulfill all righteousness. His love for the Father was manifest in His unwavering desire to live by every word that proceeded from the mouth of God. He loved the truth because He loved His Father, who is the Author of all truth.

Satan is the father of lies. He trades in untruth and does everything he can to distort, twist, or conceal the truth. Again it is the suppression of truth, specifically the truth of God, that is primary to our sinful behavior. Paul declared this in his epistle to the Romans:

> For the wrath of God is revealed from heaven against all ungodliness and unrighteousness of men, who suppress the truth in unrighteousness, because what may be known of God is manifest in them, for God has shown it to them. For since the creation of the world His invisible attributes are clearly seen, being understood by the things that are made, even His eternal power and Godhead, so that they are without excuse, because, although they knew God, they did not glorify Him as God, nor were thankful, but became futile in their thoughts, and their foolish hearts were darkened. Professing to be wise, they became fools, and changed the glory of the incorruptible God into an image made like corruptible man—and birds and four-footed animals and creeping things.
>
> Therefore God also gave them up to uncleanness, in the lusts of their hearts, to dishonor their bodies among themselves, who exchanged the truth of God for the lie, and worshiped and served the creature rather than the Creator, who is blessed forever. Amen. (1:18–25)

At the very beginning of human sin is the suppression of the truth that God reveals to all men about Himself. This general revelation clearly displays the eternal power and deity of God. But fallen human beings do not want God in their thinking. They exchange the truth of His power and deity for a lie, which propels the creature into idolatry.

Because natural humans are at enmity with God, they both hide the truth and hide themselves from the truth. God's truth elicits no joy from them. This is the opposite reaction of the one found in *agape*. True love rejoices in the truth. It wants the truth to be known and broadcast publicly. It seeks the venue of light for the truth and is not willing that it be consigned to darkness.

BEARS ALL THINGS

Paul continued:

> [Love] bears all things. (v. 7a)

Love that bears all things carries the idea in Greek of "covering in silence." The thrust is not that love illicitly covers up evil. Rather, it endures afflictions and suffering without complaint and whining. In New Testament terms, this "bearing" specifically refers to bearing persecutions that come in the wake of fidelity to Christ. It is the consequence of our justification, as Paul declared in Romans 5:

> Therefore, having been justified by faith, we have peace with God through our Lord Jesus Christ, through whom also we have access by faith into this grace in

which we stand, and rejoice in hope of the glory of
God. And not only that, but we also glory in tribulations, knowing that tribulation produces perseverance;
and perseverance, character; and character, hope. Now
hope does not disappoint, because the love of God has
been poured out in our hearts by the Holy Spirit who
was given to us. (vv. 1–5)

The fruits of justification include peace with God, access to His
gracious presence, and joy in our hope. Beyond these, Paul spoke
of an ability to glory in tribulations. It is because the love of God
has been poured out in our hearts that even tribulation can become
an occasion for glory. These words of the Apostle echo the benediction Jesus conferred on those who are persecuted for His sake:
"Blessed are those who are persecuted for righteousness' sake, for
theirs is the kingdom of heaven. Blessed are you when they revile
and persecute you, and say all kinds of evil against you falsely for
My sake. Rejoice and be exceedingly glad, for great is your reward
in heaven, for so they persecuted the prophets who were before
you" (Matt. 5:10–12).

The blessing of God is poured out on those who suffer for the
sake of Christ. They are promised the possession of the kingdom. In
the same manner, those who must bear such calumny are promised
a great reward in heaven. Because of the appointed ends of these
sufferings, we are called on not only to bear them but also to see
them as occasions for joy and exceeding gladness. The glorious
rewards promised those who love Christ enough to bear all things
are accented in the Apocalypse of John:

To him who overcomes I will give to eat from the tree of life, which is in the midst of the Paradise of God.

And to the angel of the church in Smyrna write, "These things says the First and the Last, who was dead, and came to life: 'I know your works, tribulation, and poverty (but you are rich); and I know the blasphemy of those who say they are Jews and are not, but are a synagogue of Satan. Do not fear any of those things which you are about to suffer. Indeed, the devil is about to throw some of you into prison, that you may be tested, and you will have tribulation ten days. Be faithful until death, and I will give you the crown of life.'" (Rev. 2:7–10)

The promises given to the churches include the privilege of eating from the tree of life, the crown of life, freedom from harm from the second death, the hidden manna, and the white stone with a new name on it (vv. 17–18). Finally, the faithful church in Philadelphia is promised the following:

And to the angel of the church in Philadelphia write, "These things says He who is holy, He who is true, 'He who has the key of David, He who opens and no one shuts, and shuts and no one opens': 'I know your works. See, I have set before you an open door, and no one can shut it; for you have a little strength, have kept My word, and have not denied My name. Indeed I will make those of the synagogue of Satan, who say they are Jews and are not, but lie—indeed I will make them come and worship before your feet, and to know that I have loved you. Because you have kept My command to persevere, I also will keep you from the hour of trial which shall come upon the whole world, to test those who dwell on the earth. Behold, I am coming quickly! Hold fast what you have, that no one may take your crown. He who overcomes, I will make him a pillar in the temple of My God, and he shall go out no more. I will write on him the name of My God and the name of the city of My God, the New Jerusalem, which comes down out of heaven from My God. And I will write on him My new name.

'He who has an ear, let him hear what the Spirit says to the churches.'" (Rev. 3:7–13)

These promises drip with the overflow of the abundance of glory that is stored up for the saints who persevere in bearing the afflictions that come with being identified with Christ. They reflect the price tag and the reward of love.

BELIEVES, HOPES, ENDURES ALL THINGS

Finally, Paul said:

[Love] believes all things, hopes all things, endures all things. (v. 7b)

To believe all things is not to indulge in credulity. They are fools who believe everything they read or hear. This is not a call to an uncritical acceptance of every assertion we encounter. The point is that love believes all things that are spoken by God. We embrace the Word of God as true.

The bitter controversy over the authority and integrity of the Bible that has divided the church the past two centuries is not simply an academic dispute over inspiration or inerrancy. The debate also touches heavily on the issue of love. The people of God love the Word of God and place their trust in its veracity. Their posture is not one of unbelief.

As a student, I was exposed to relentless criticism and skepticism of the Bible by many of my seminary professors. In a private conversation with one of them, I said: "One thing I observe among you and your associates is that you seem to take delight in leveling your attacks against Scripture. You express your criticisms with glee. It seems to me that a Christian, forced by incontrovertible evidence to abandon his confession in the trustworthiness of the Bible, would do it with tears."

It is noteworthy that throughout Paul's exposition of love he not only distinguished among faith, hope, and love, but also linked them to show that they remain connected and mutually dependent on each other. The biblical concept of hope does not lack the confidence that is missing from our cultural concept of hope. In normal conversations, the term *hope* indicates a desire for a reality that may not come to pass. The biblical concept does not hang suspended in such uncertainty. Rather, hope is faith confidently looking forward to the future. It is a hope that will not disappoint or leave us ashamed. It is the anchor of the soul that gives stability to the Christian life.

If there is a person or a power in this world that has great endurance, we can hope for its long-term continuity. But if its staying power is limited, sooner or later it will lose its efficacy and falter. As its strength erodes, it finally succumbs to failure. However, if a force is able not only to endure most things but, in fact, endures *all* things, then it follows necessarily that it will never fail.

NEVER FAILS

Paul, indeed, affirmed that love is unfailing:

> Love never fails. But whether there are prophecies, they will fail; whether there are tongues, they will cease; whether there is knowledge, it will vanish away. For we know in part and we prophesy in part. But when that which is perfect has come, then that which is in part will be done away. (vv. 8–10)

It is hard for us to conceive of something that never fails. Our greatest heroes all fail at some point. Our electronic gadgets promise long life but grow dim and wear out. Our greatest champions do not win every contest. But love is a champion that boasts an unblemished record. It is undefeated in every contest. It never fails. In this respect, love differs from the other gifts Paul described in 1 Corinthians. In contrast to prophecy, tongues, and knowledge, love stands alone as the one that will endure through the ages.

Paul actually gave a time frame in which prophecies will fail, tongues will cease, and knowledge will vanish. This startling declaration has provoked much debate among scholars. At issue is the question of when these other gifts will pass away. Was Paul saying these gifts will cease at the final consummation of the kingdom of Christ? Was he speaking of something that would occur in redemptive history at the death of the last Apostle? Did he see this happening at the completion of the writing of the New Testament? What did he mean?

Paul said these gifts will cease when "that which is perfect has come." Is this "perfect" the final state of things at the return of Christ? Or does it refer to something that is "completed" before that happens? Those who are cessationists, who believe that the miraculous gifts that were evident in the Apostolic era are no longer functioning today, argue that Paul was referring to the completion of the New Testament. They think Paul was saying that after the completion of the Apostolic word, the divine revelation of Scripture, the temporary and local prophecies would give way to the normative written word.

The text does not answer this question explicitly. For our concerns at the moment, to understand *agape*, the answer does not matter much. What does matter is that we grasp and gain the kind of love that outlasts these other gifts.

FROM CHILDHOOD TO MATURITY

Paul added to his admonition:

> When I was a child, I spoke as a child, I understood as
> a child, I thought as a child; but when I became a man,
> I put away childish things. For now we see in a mirror,
> dimly, but then face to face. Now I know in part, but
> then I shall know just as I also am known. (vv. 11–12)

Paul used the analogy of growing up from childhood to adulthood. He noted that the passage involves serious changes in speech, understanding, and thinking. Here we see the stark contrast between a *childlike* faith and a *childish* faith. Christians are called to be mature in their manner of speaking, thinking, and understanding. We no longer speak in "baby talk." We are not to think in simplistic terms as children do. Indeed, we are to go beyond childhood and past adolescence to full maturity.

We see children going about carrying their favorite blankets or teddy bears, which they grasp tightly for security. They are cute to behold, but they are, in reality, childish. There is nothing wrong with children using childish things. Their toys are designed for their age and maturity levels. But when adulthood arrives, we are not to continue playing with dolls and teddy bears. We are to put these things aside and embrace the tools of adulthood. The chief tool of adulthood is *agape*. We can never embrace it too soon. We are never too old to rely on it.

Our present perception of heavenly things is at best blurred. We delight in the partial knowledge that God's revelation affords us now, but it is not worthy to be compared with that which He has stored up for us in heaven. It is like looking at ourselves in a polished bronze mirror. The bronze gives an image but not a clear one. We must remember that the mirror Paul described here did not have the sharpness of image that modern mirrors afford.

Dimness will give way to acute perception. We will move out of our present cave, where we behold shadows dancing on the walls around us, and into the noonday sun. We will see the unveiled glory of God and the full exaltation of Christ. We will enjoy our friends and relatives in a way that transcends beyond imagination our enjoyment of them in this world. Our friends and loved ones will be all the more lovely because all remnants of their and our sins and imperfections will be gone. Likewise, our love for them will be undiluted and pure in its expression. We will know and be known in a way that triumphs over all distortion and concealment, and in all these things the driving force of our sanctification will be a perfecting love. Not only will we know as we are being known, but we shall love as we are being loved. The childish will give way to the mature, and the partial will surrender to the complete.

THE GREATEST IS LOVE

Paul concluded this Apostolic exposition by again linking the three great graces: faith, hope, and love:

> And now abide faith, hope love, these three; but the
> greatest of these is love. (v. 13)

How central is faith to the gospel and the Apostolic teaching? It is by faith that the Christian appropriates all of the benefits of the ministry of Christ. Without faith it is impossible to please God (Heb. 11:6). Faith is a necessary condition for salvation. It is hard therefore to minimize its importance. Nay, its importance must never be minimized, as it is essential to Christianity.

Likewise, it is of vast importance that we maintain the essential character of hope as it is linked to our faith. We trust God for what He has accomplished for us not only in the past, but in hope we trust Him completely for the future. Without hope, we are like ships without rudders, tossed to and fro with every wind and buffeted without stability in an unbelieving and hostile world.

Paul did not denigrate faith and hope in stressing the supreme importance of love. He assured us that all three, the full triad of Christian virtues, will abide. They will not perish or shrink into insignificance. But the one virtue that is elevated to the superlative level is love.

Faith, hope, and love are all great. But in this triad, there is one that is the greatest of the great—the gift and virtue of love.

NOTES

1. Jonathan Edwards, *Charity and Its Fruits* (Edinburgh: Banner of Truth, 1969), 68–69.
2. Edwards, *Charity and Its Fruits*, 187.

CONCLUSION

OF THE FATHER'S
LOVE BEGOTTEN

In our analysis of the love of God, we have sought to scale the heights of that which is virtually unscalable. When God reveals Himself to us, He must stoop down and, as John Calvin said, lisp to us, as parents speak to their infant children. We long for the concrete that will make the abstract clear, the narrative that will boldly illustrate the didactic.

If there is any such concrete narrative that sets forth the love of the Father by which we have become His begotten and adopted children, it is the parable of the prodigal son. We recall that Jesus did not give this story a formal title. The title "parable of the prodigal son" is an invention of Bible translators who supply chapter and paragraph headings in the text of Scripture for our facility. Since the parable follows the parable of the lost coin and the parable of the lost sheep, some have titled it "the parable of the lost son."

Other titles could legitimately be used for this story. It could be called "the parable of the jealous brother" because of the featured role of the elder brother, who resented the celebration given at the homecoming of his wayward sibling. One other title would also be fitting: "the parable of the loving father." The actions of the father in this story are every bit as important for us to understand as the actions of the two sons. Let us look briefly at the parable:

> Then He said: "A certain man had two sons. And the younger of them said to his father, 'Father, give me the portion of goods that falls to me.' So he divided to them his livelihood. And not many days after, the younger son gathered all together, journeyed to a far country, and there wasted his possessions with prodigal living. But when he had spent all, there arose a severe famine in that land, and he began to be in want. Then he went and joined himself to a citizen of that country, and he sent him into his fields to feed swine. And he would gladly have filled his stomach with the pods that the swine ate, and no one gave him anything.
>
> "But when he came to himself, he said, 'How many of my father's hired servants have bread enough and to spare, and I perish with hunger! I will arise and go to my father, and will say to him, "Father, I have sinned against heaven and before you, and I am no

longer worthy to be called your son. Make me like one of your hired servants.'"

"And he arose and came to his father. But when he was still a great way off, his father saw him and had compassion, and ran and fell on his neck and kissed him. And the son said to him, 'Father, I have sinned against heaven and in your sight, and am no longer worthy to be called your son.'

"But the father said to his servants, 'Bring out the best robe and put it on him, and put a ring on his hand and sandals on his feet. And bring the fatted calf here and kill it, and let us eat and be merry; for this my son was dead and is alive again; he was lost and is found.' And they began to be merry.

"Now his older son was in the field. And as he came and drew near to the house, he heard music and dancing. So he called one of the servants and asked what these things meant. And he said to him, 'Your brother has come, and because he has received him safe and sound, your father has killed the fatted calf.'

"But he was angry and would not go in. Therefore his father came out and pleaded with him. So he answered and said to his father, 'Lo, these many years I have been serving you; I never transgressed your commandment at any time; and yet you never gave me a young goat, that I might make merry with my friends. But as soon as this son of yours came, who has devoured your livelihood with harlots, you killed the fatted calf for him.'

> "And he said to him, 'Son, you are always with me,
> and all that I have is yours. It was right that we should
> make merry and be glad, for your brother was dead
> and is alive again, and was lost and is found.'" (Luke
> 15:11–32)

This story features a profligate young man who, in his impetuosity, had no patience for delayed gratification. He wanted his inheritance right away. His father acquiesced to his pleas and gave him what he desired. Surely the father understood the folly of his son's request. His granting of it was not an act of parental weakness but of wisdom and courage. Sometimes it is necessary for loving parents to let their children go out on their own even when it is obvious that they are neither mature nor trustworthy.

I live in Florida, where the beaches are a major venue for the annual American ritual known as "spring break." Each year, in March and April, tens of thousands of college students head south to stage an unrestrained modern version of the ancient bacchanalia. Orgies of sex, drunkenness, and wild pranks mark the behavior of young people who would be loath to behave in such an unrestrained manner at home or even on their university campuses. But, like the prodigal son, they go to a far country, a place where they are unknown, where the cloak of anonymity can conceal their wantonness from exposure to family and friends.

The prodigal son's "spring break" ended in disaster. After his money was depleted, he was not able to wire home for more. He ended up living in a pigsty, sharing quarters with the swine, and was so hungry that he coveted the slop he fed the pigs.

While he was in this state of total degeneration, the young man "came to himself." He was convicted of his sin and resolved to return to his father in humility and repentance. He was determined to make no further claims of sonship, but would plead to be allowed to return to his father's house as a hired servant.

The father saw his son approaching in the distance. Jesus said that the father had compassion and ran to his son. In the ancient world, the common attire for men was an ankle-length robe. In order for males to run freely, they had to "gird up their loins." This meant hiking up the robe above the knees and then fastening it with a belt so the legs would be free to pump quickly. We see the prodigal's father running down the road, with bared knees pumping, in order to greet his son. The greeting had no rebuke, no stern reprimand for wasting the father's goods. Rather, he fell on his son's neck and kissed him.

Jesus described the meeting in terms of passionate affection. The father held nothing back in the expression of his love. Still, the son cowered in penance, expressing his unworthiness, but the father would have none of it. He would not subject his son to the status of a slave. Instead, he commanded that his son be fully restored to the family and made ready to celebrate the event with a magnificent feast. He clothed his son in the best robe and put a ring on his finger and sandals on his feet. The fatted calf was slain that the family might rejoice and make merry.

Such is the love of God. Such is the love of our heavenly Father, who takes us from the pigsty and robes us in the righteousness of Christ. He gives us the signet ring of His own family and puts shoes on our feet. His forgiveness is not reluctant but festive, as together with the angels in heaven He makes merry with us.

Oh, the depth and the riches of this love …

ABOUT THE AUTHOR

Dr. R. C. Sproul is the founder and chairman of Ligonier Ministries, an international Christian education ministry based near Orlando, Florida. He also serves as senior minister of preaching and teaching at Saint Andrew's, a Reformed congregation in Sanford, Florida, and as the president of Reformation Bible College. His teaching can be heard on the daily radio program *Renewing Your Mind.*

During his distinguished academic career, Dr. Sproul helped train men for the ministry as a professor at several theological seminaries.

He is the author of more than eighty books, including *The Holiness of God, Chosen by God, The Invisible Hand, Faith Alone, A Taste of Heaven, Truths We Confess, The Truth of the Cross,* and *The Prayer of the Lord.* He also served as general editor of *The Reformation Study Bible* and has written several children's books, including *The Prince's Poison Cup.*

Dr. Sproul and his wife, Vesta, make their home in Longwood, Florida.

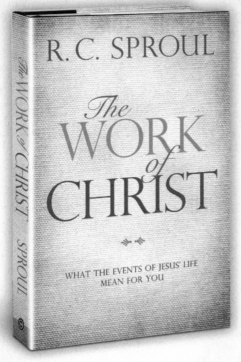